LAW, FOREIGN POLICY, AND
THE EAST-WEST *DÉTENTE*

Law, Foreign Policy, and the East-West *Détente*

Edited by

EDWARD McWHINNEY

Professor of Law
University of Toronto

UNIVERSITY OF TORONTO PRESS

Foreword

THIS VOLUME has its roots in the Conference on Law and World Affairs, held in the Faculty of Law of the University of Toronto on January 17 and 18, 1964, under the general title, "The Soviet-Western *Détente*: Cold War to Co-existence?" A number of the essays in the present volume stem from papers delivered at the Conference. These particular papers have been substantially rewritten and revised for the purpose of publication as essays in permanent, book form. The remaining essays have been specially commissioned to round out the analysis and discussion.

The basic theme of this collection of essays is the response of the West in general, and of Canada in particular, to the far-reaching changes in Soviet external relations in the last several years, as reflected in the current apparent East-West *détente* following from the peaceful resolution of the October, 1962, crisis and also in the successful achievement of the Moscow Partial Test Ban Treaty of August, 1963. The volume begins with an analysis of the changes in Soviet internal life in the era of de-Stalinization, for these internal changes necessarily condition and affect, in measure, the practical conduct of foreign policy. It continues with an examination of distinctive Soviet theories of international law and relations, and their impact on and significance for classical, Western-based theories and Western policy-making in general. The emphasis then shifts to more specifically Canadian questions, focussing on concrete Canadian responses to Soviet moves in international arenas like the United Nations General Assembly and special committees and agencies, such as the Sixth (Legal) Committee and the International Law Commission, and also in authoritative, if private, scientific, and non-governmental bodies like the International Law Association. In this vein, the latter essays in the volume look to the opportunities presented for independent Canadian initiatives in East-West relations, in the light of the changes in the Soviet Union and the Soviet bloc generally. The volume concludes with an essay, from the Soviet viewpoint, on the possibilities, in the present era, for co-existence and co-operation among states with different social systems.

Our task would not be complete if we did not take the opportunity here of acknowledging the kind assistance, advice, or counsel, accorded in various ways in connection with the present project, by Claude T. Bissell, Cecil A. Wright, Bora Laskin, Ernest Sirluck, John Holmes, the Hon. Paul Martin, Marcel Cadieux, and Arnold Smith. In addition, Fred H. Zemans as chairman of the Students' Committee, John M. Roland, Fred G. Gans, Marc J. Somerville, J. Garnet Pink, Robert A. Shea, J. Allen Karp, Fred A. Stewart, and Jay B. Waterman undertook the organization and administration of the Conference on Law and World Affairs, and so, by the same token, contributed to the materialization of this volume which, in its basic theme and ideas, derives in such large measure from the intellectual exchanges and discussions at that conference. Miss Carole Harris of the Office of the Faculty of Law, University of Toronto, has typed all the manuscript, and otherwise assisted in the organization of the materials.

We should also like to thank the Canadian Institute of International Affairs for its helpful interest in distribution of the book.

March 2, 1964   EDWARD MCWHINNEY

Contents

LAW, FOREIGN POLICY, AND THE EAST-WEST *DÉTENTE*

Soviet Law Reform and its Significance for Soviet International Relations

HAROLD J. BERMAN

IT IS FITTING that we discuss—in the same breath, as it were—both the Soviet legal system and Soviet international relations.

At first the two subjects seem to be only remotely connected. What has the new Russian Criminal Code, or the Comrades' Courts, to do with Berlin or Cuba? Yet if we go deeper we realize that the problem of getting along, somehow, with the Soviets, the problem of creating peace on this planet, requires the development of techniques of international negotiation, administration, adjudication, and legislation—essentially legal techniques; and not only the development of techniques but also the development of standards of international justice, principles of international order, which are closely related to standards and principles of contract law, tort law, criminal law, property law, administrative law, constitutional law, and other branches of the legal tree.

Someone has said that the lawyer's art is the art of the

impossible, the art of reconciling opposites, of squaring the circle. Peace is precarious in today's world partly because we have not yet found the techniques and institutions whereby the crucial conflicts between the communist and the non-communist world may be overcome. Whether we think of those conflicts essentially in terms of a power struggle between Uncle Sam and Mother Russia, or in terms of an ideological struggle between revolutionary Marxism and liberal democracy, or in terms of a culture-struggle between East and West—we need procedures and principles for reducing the conflicts, for keeping them within bounds short of open warfare, and also for building areas of co-operation which may one day resolve the conflicts. And that means we need law.

But then the critical question is posed: Can we find a common law upon which to build a peaceful world? Do Soviet ideas of law have enough in common with Western ideas of law to provide a mutually acceptable system for reducing and resolving conflict? We cannot answer this question without analysing both the similarities and the differences between Soviet conceptions of law and our own.

At the same time, the links between Soviet international relations and Soviet internal law must themselves be seen on the still broader background of the interplay between Soviet international relations and Soviet internal political, economic, and social developments. There are, of course, pitfalls to be avoided in attempting to relate foreign policy to domestic policy; it cannot simply be assumed that a régime which is oppressive to its own people will necessarily be hostile toward other peoples, or that a régime which is liberal and democratic at home will inevitably be friendly and tractable abroad. Yet in the case of the Soviet Union, "Stalinism" meant both despotism internally and Cold War internationally, and not only we but also the Soviets themselves often associate Khrushchev's denunciations of Stalinism with a more liberal, more humane, and democratic domestic policy, and, at the same time, with a more peaceful foreign policy.

For many years it has been unpopular, however, among Western experts on the Soviet Union to be optimistic with respect to "de-Stalinization," both domestic and international. It has been much more popular, and much safer, to be pessimistic or even cynical. Indeed, a "realistic" view is often equated with the most gloomy estimates and forecasts, while those who emphasize the steps which the Soviet Union has taken, and is taking, in the direction of a greater liberalization of its social order and a more peaceful and law-respecting foreign policy are often labelled "naive."

Ten years ago it was the "realistic" view of leading Western specialists on Soviet affairs that the Soviet system was bound to become progressively more despotic and oppressive. This was considered an iron law of totalitarianism. It was said that the Soviet dictatorship must continually increase its terrorism in order to deal with the continually increasing dissatisfaction of the people it oppresses. This "realistic" theory has now been disproved; for one thing, it failed to take into account the fact that the death of the dictator might affect the situation. Today, "realism" postulates a cyclical theory; the post-Stalin era is represented as a "breathing-spell," to be followed by a new Stalinism. The Soviet political system is depicted as a "pendulum" which periodically swings from terror to relaxation and back to terror. Indeed, swings of the pendulum are detected almost every year. Yet more than a decade has passed since Stalin's death and no new Stalin is in sight, nor has the general direction of Soviet domestic policy shifted substantially.

It would, of course, be foolish not to recognize that a return to Stalinism in the Soviet Union at some future time is possible. I shall discuss this possibility later. But this is very different from saying that it is probable, let alone imminent or inevitable as many "realists" have insisted.

In the realm of Soviet foreign policy, "realism" supposed, after 1948, that Stalin would invade Yugoslavia. "Realism" also denied the possibility that the Soviet government would ever withdraw its troops from Austria. "Realism" first included Communist China in the "Soviet bloc" and then spoke of the "Sino-Soviet bloc," without taking into account the fact that communism, as a faith, had already eroded to the point that it was incapable of holding together countries whose fundamental interests were in conflict. "Realism" contended that the Soviets were not interested in foreign trade but only in economic autarchy, although we can now see that annual Soviet exports and imports have increased in the past fifteen years from about two billion dollars to about fifteen billion dollars. Similarly, "realism" doubted that the Soviets would ever agree, even in principle, to any kind of inspection of disarmament or arms control.

Indeed, again and again, pessimistic views about the Soviet Union, advanced in the name of realism, have proved to be the naive ones. This has not overly disturbed us, nor has it brought pessimism in this field into disrepute, probably because there is a certain psychological comfort in having one's worst fears proved groundless, whereas to discover that one's fondest hopes were but illusions is frustrating in the extreme. We cannot forget the cruel disappointment of the dreams of a future Soviet-American friendship which were engendered during World War II. Yet the excessive optimism of the wartime period does not justify the excessive pessimism of the postwar reaction.

Unquestionably we should avoid all "isms," including both pessimism and optimism. But we should not abandon hope—hope, in particular, that the Russian Revolution which started in November, 1917, has settled down, has lost much of its revolutionary dogmatism in domestic policy and much of its revolutionary virulence abroad. This hope has ample support in the events not only of the past decade but also of the past three decades. It is this hope that justifies us in seeking to establish a lasting framework of peaceful economic, cultural, and political relations with the Soviet Union. At the same time, the very effort to establish such a lasting framework of peaceful relations can itself help to bring this hope to fruition.

To say that much of the dogmatism and virulence of the Bolshevik Revolution has been lost in the past three decades is not to say that the road to peace is broad and straight and smooth; on the contrary, everything I have said thus far presupposes that it is narrow and crooked and rough. The Soviet leaders have different ideas about the world we live in from those of our leaders; they have different interests, different aims. At many points those differences are so sharp as to present the gravest obstacles to peace. Yet it is important that we do not confuse the Soviet ideas, interests, and policies of today with those of fifteen, thirty, or forty-five years ago. Today the Soviet Union, the second most powerful nation in the world, has established an enormous network of intricate relationships —political, economic, and cultural—with scores of other nations, nations representing a very wide variety of attitudes towards the Soviet Union. Conceivably it would be in the Soviet interest for the whole world to be communist; yet conceivably it would not (where would the capital of such a communist world be located?—in New York?—in Peking?); at any rate, for the foreseeable future, the Soviet Union has a very strong interest in preserving the stability of those international relationships which are relatively favourable to it and in preventing the others from deteriorating still further. This means that it has a very strong interest in preserving international law. Indeed, international law has proved its immediate utility to Soviet foreign policy again and again—at the time of the U-2 flight in 1960, at the time of the attack upon Egypt in 1956, and at many other times.

It is often said, however, that the Soviets will respect international law only when it is in their interests to do so. To a certain extent this is true; indeed, to a certain extent it is true of all countries, for international law rests ultimately on consent, and no country will agree to sacrifice its own *ultimate* interests to international legal standards. The deeper question is to what extent a country sees its own interests in terms of the preservation of the international legal order.

It is, indeed, in the interests of the Soviet Union—and it is so recognized by the Soviet leadership—to observe certain aspects of international law fairly rigorously. International legal rules relating to territorial integrity, jurisdiction, freedom of the seas, and other prerequisites of sovereignty, are generally respected by the Soviet Union, partly because of its political interest in avoiding excessive friction with other nations. International legal rules relating to commercial transactions—particularly the export and import of goods —are honoured by the Soviets, partly because the Soviet Union has strong economic interest in maintaining foreign trade on stable and calculable foundations.

From the fact that the Soviets will observe international law when it is to their advantage to do so, we should not draw the pessimistic conclusion that Soviet adherence to international law is worthless. Rather we should ask, "How can we help make it more and more to their advantage to observe international law?" "How can we influence them to think in terms not only of their own advantage but also of their mutual advantage with others?"

Yet, ultimately, international law must rest on more than

advantage, and on more, even, than mutual advantage; for the criterion of advantage suggests a degree of instability which itself contradicts the concept of law.

Does it, however, contradict the *Soviet* concept of law? American specialists on Soviet affairs are fond of quoting Lenin's statement that "Law is politics" (or "policy"—the word is the same in Russian, *politika*). If law is politics (as not only Lenin but also Aristotle said), can one speak of subordinating political interests to law or even of conceiving political interests in terms of law?

A quotation from a leading Soviet jurist, G. I. Tunkin, on the relationship between politics and law in the international field has importance in this connection. Professor Tunkin, who is Chief Legal Adviser of the Soviet Ministry of Foreign Affairs, wrote in 1956:

International law, together with the fact that it represents a combination of principles and norms binding upon states, is, like any law, a weapon of policy: both socialist and capitalist states in carrying out their foreign policy make more or less use of international law. From this, however, it certainly does not follow that international law can be a weapon of any policy. Generally recognized principles and norms of contemporary international law, being in their essence democratic, may be used as a weapon of the foreign policy of states only within the limits defined by the content of those norms.

Tunkin's reformulation of the Leninist doctrine must be read not only in the light of Soviet theories of international law but also in the light of Soviet theories of domestic law. For the view that "law is [only] politics" haunted Soviet legal developments in the first twenty years of the development of the Soviet state. It was only in 1937 and 1938 that it came to be seen by Soviet jurists, and by Stalin himself, that the stability of the state itself depends not only on politics but also on law, and that law, as Vyshinsky wrote in 1938, "cannot be reduced to politics."

SINCE 1917 Soviet law has advanced and receded in successive waves; yet each advance has gone farther than the preceding one.

The period from 1917 to 1921 was one of revolutionary nihilism, civil war, and loosely organized terror. The period from 1921 to 1928 was conceived as a temporary retreat to legality. Then from 1929 to 1936 came a resurgence of the original militancy, accompanied by an attack upon legal institutions. From 1937 on, however, Stalin established a dual state: "stability of laws" and "socialist legality" were proclaimed and made applicable to those areas of Soviet life where the political factor was stabilized, while terror, either naked or in the guise of law (as in the purge trials of the late 1930's), was applied where the régime felt itself threatened.

A month after Stalin's death in March, 1953, his successors began to proclaim the "inviolability" of Soviet law and to denounce "arbitrary procedures" and "violations of socialist legality," particularly in connection with the so-called "Doctors' Plot," which many have supposed Stalin trumped up in the last months of his life as a pretext for a new wave of purges. After the arrest of Beria in July, 1953, many of the excesses of Stalinist terror were attributed not to the dictator himself but to his chief of secret police. This description wore thin, however, and in February, 1956, Khrushchev attacked Stalin by name at the Twentieth Congress of the Communist Party of the Soviet Union, denouncing him for the "cult of personality" and for persecution of loyal party members in violation of their legal rights. In October-November, 1961, at the Twenty-Second Party Congress, the attacks on Stalin were renewed with even greater vigour. The inviolability of socialist law was again proclaimed. Vyshinsky's name was added to Stalin's as co-author of a legal system which permitted falsification and distortion of legality for the persecution of people innocent of any crime.

In implementation of these attacks upon the "cult of personality," important steps have been taken since September, 1953, to eliminate those features of the pre-existing Soviet law which permitted the disguise of terror in legal form.

First, the Special Board of the Ministry of Internal Affairs has been abolished. It was this Special Board which had been the chief instrument of terror. It was a three-man administrative committee—the Russians called it a *troika*—which was empowered by a 1934 statute to send people to labour camps without a hearing, in a secret administrative procedure, without right of counsel and without right of appeal.

Second, the security police have been deprived of the power to conduct investigations of crimes under their own special rules without supervision of the Procuracy.

Third, the special procedures for court cases involving the most serious anti-state crimes have been abolished. The laws of 1934 and 1937 permitting persons charged with certain such crimes to be tried secretly, in absentia, and without counsel, were repealed.

Fourth, the military courts, which had previously had a wide jurisdiction over civilians, particularly in the case of political crimes, have been deprived of all jurisdiction over civilians except for espionage.

Fifth, the law permitting punishment of relatives of one who deserts to a foreign country from the armed forces—though they knew nothing of the desertion—has been abolished.

Sixth, Vyshinsky's doctrine that confessions have special evidentiary force in cases of counter-revolutionary crimes—based on the transparently false notion that people will not confess to such crimes unless they are actually guilty—

has been repudiated; confessions are now treated as having no evidentiary force in themselves, and the matters contained in a confession must be corroborated by other evidence.

Seventh, Vyshinsky's doctrine that the burden of proof shifts to the accused in cases of counter-revolutionary crimes has also been repudiated. The new Soviet codes place the burden of proving the guilt of the accused squarely on the prosecutor. Although the phrase "presumption of innocence" is avoided in the codes, all that we mean by that phrase is spelled out in Soviet law.

Eighth, Vyshinsky's broad definition of complicity, borrowed from the Anglo-American doctrine of conspiracy, has been repudiated. Innocent association with others who are planning an illegal act can no longer constitute a crime under the new Soviet legislation.

Ninth, the law on so-called "counter-revolutionary crimes" has been slightly narrowed and made a little less vague. The term "counter-revolutionary" has been eliminated and the term "anti-state" substituted. The law on state secrets has been substantially relaxed—though it is still far wider in its scope than we would consider tolerable. And a new list of information constituting state secrets has been enacted which is less broad and more precise than the earlier list.

Finally, there took place from 1953 (or 1955) to 1957 a systematic re-examination of all cases of persons previously convicted of counter-revolutionary crimes and the release from labour camps of the overwhelming majority of such persons as fully rehabilitated.

The restoration of procedural due process of law in political cases is a signal achievement of the post-Stalin régime. The Soviet citizen is now protected against police terror, false charges, and faked trials to a far greater extent than ever before in Soviet history. No longer need he fear the midnight knock on the door as a prelude to transportation to a Siberian labour camp without a fair hearing.

Yet one cannot speak of the total elimination of political terror so long as open opposition to Communist Party policy—the "Party line"—can lead to criminal sanctions, however "objectively" and "correctly" imposed. The 1958 Statute on State Crimes carries over from the earlier law on counter-revolutionary crimes the provisions against "agitation or propaganda" directed against the Soviet System. To defame the Soviet political and social system, or even to possess written materials of such defamatory nature, if for the purpose of weakening Soviet authority, is punishable by deprivation of freedom not exceeding seven years. In 1961, for example, certain leaders of the Jewish community in Leningrad were convicted of the crime of circulating anti-Soviet literature from a foreign embassy, presumably the Israeli. We would call this a denial of "substantive" due process of law.

The law of anti-state agitation and propaganda is only one of many features of the Soviet system which keep alive the fear of Soviet citizens that the terror may return. The fear of a return to terror is itself a form of terror. Therefore, one must view the developments of the past ten years as reflecting only a tendency—though an extremely important tendency—towards the elimination of terror.

Even apart from political crimes, Soviet law has undergone substantial liberalization in the past ten years. It would be impossible to list the hundreds, indeed thousands, of needed reforms which have been introduced. Let me speak very briefly of some of the most important, first in criminal law and procedure, then in criminal punishment and the system of detention, and finally in some other fields of law.

In criminal law and procedure, the "tightening up" of the

rules with respect to burden of proof, evaluation of confessions, and the doctrine of complicity, which have already been mentioned in the discussion of political crimes, have given increased protection to persons accused of other crimes as well. In addition, the right to counsel prior to trial, though still limited, has been significantly extended; the time for supervisory review of acquittals in criminal cases, formerly unlimited, has been reduced to one year; powers of search and seizure have been somewhat restricted; the doctrine of analogy, whereby a person who committed a socially dangerous act not specifically made punishable by law could be sentenced under a law proscribing an analogous act, has been eliminated; penalties have been substantially lightened for many crimes—for example, new laws imposing lighter sentences for petty rowdyism ("hooliganism") and petty theft of state or public property have removed the necessity of many long years in labour camps for conviction on trivial offences; and some crimes have been eliminated altogether—for example, abortion, absenteeism from work, and quitting one's job without permission. The large-scale amnesties of 1953 and 1957 released all except those sentenced for, or charged with, the most serious offences.

With respect to the system of detention, a 1957 law eliminated the name "labour camp," substituting "labour colony" for all places of confinement (except prisons, which are used only for temporary detention or, very rarely, for the most serious crimes) and introduced a new régime for prisoners which permits far more leniency in their treatment. Those convicted of less serious crimes are permitted to have their wives (or husbands) visit and stay with them from time to time; they are paid substantial wages for their work and are required to send home allotments to their dependents. Also, liberal parole provisions have been introduced.

Liberalization has not been confined to criminal policy. Since 1953, and especially since 1955, there has been a re-examination of every branch of law and a weeding out of many of the harshest features. For example, a new civil right has been created to obtain a court order for public retraction of a newspaper libel. Equal rights of foreigners under Soviet law have been declared—subject, of course, to statutory restrictions. (It would be interesting to put those two provisions together and to have a suit by a foreigner in a Soviet court demanding a retraction of a newspaper libel against him.) In labour law the rights of trade unions have been enhanced and the procedures for settlement of workers' grievances have been improved. In family law, a new code has been drafted which, among other things, ameliorates the position of the child born out of wedlock. Similar examples could be multiplied from many other fields of law.

Since 1961 there has been a contrary trend, away from liberalization, in certain areas. Harsh criminal and administrative penalties have been imposed upon persons who constitute "anti-social, parasitic elements" and who are not performing socially useful work but are living on unearned income. The death penalty has been extended to a wide variety of crimes, many of them economic crimes not involving violence. Despite these backward steps, however, the liberal momentum of the post-Stalin reforms has not stopped. Indeed, the law reforms have already been counted. A vast structure of procedures and rights has been built, and though its foundations need to be strengthened, it is not something which can easily be toppled.

IT SHOULD BE APPARENT from the above analysis that although the liberalization of Soviet law in the past ten years has not been an unbroken forward movement, nevertheless, "the thaw" (as the Soviet writer Ehrenburg called it in 1954) has continued and still continues. There has been a substantial reduction of terror, a substantial increase in freedom to criticize, greater encouragement of individual initiative, and a relaxation of tensions. From the point of view of personal rights and freedoms, there is an enormous difference between the Russia of eleven years ago and the Russia of today.

Nevertheless, there remains the long-range problem of whether the Soviet leaders are willing and able to establish not merely a new policy of freedom, but also a legal and institutional foundation which will make freedom secure from their own intervention. Until they do so, the possibility —and the fear—of a return to Stalinism will continue to exist.

The United States and other Western countries should respond to this situation by doing everything possible to encourage the establishment of conditions in which Soviet legality, and protection of personal rights, will be strengthened. Of course, it is not easy for any country so to conduct its foreign policy as to influence the internal development of another country—especially when the outlook and interests of the two countries clash at many points. Nevertheless, we must recognize that our foreign policy does in fact have an influence on Soviet internal development.

In particular, by doing what we can to relax international tensions and maintain more friendly relations with the Soviet Union, we help to foster stable conditions within the Soviet Union and thus to give personal rights and freedoms a better chance to develop. In addition, by establishing extensive economic and cultural relations with the Soviet Union, we help to strengthen the hand of those Soviet citizens who seek to consolidate personal rights in their own country.

By the same token, our refusal to give due credit for the progress of the past decade is frustrating to those who are responsible for that progress. Our wholesale denunciations of the Soviet system, which fail to distinguish between its real vices and its real virtues, only add to the hardship of those Soviet citizens who are attempting to reduce its vices and increase its virtues.

The West can only welcome Soviet law reform as a hopeful sign for the building of an enduring framework of peaceful relations in the international sphere, recognizing that our own evaluation of Soviet developments can have a strong influence on those developments. If we give up hope of a gradual transformation of communism from within, we are led to take steps that make such a transformation more difficult. Similarly, if we insist that because of Soviet intentions a lasting peace is impossible, we help to confirm those intentions and to make peace impossible. Since the Soviet situation depends in part on us, any prophecy we make tends to be self-fulfilling. In these circumstances, we owe it to ourselves to err, if we must err at all, on the side of optimism rather than of pessimism.

Co-existence, Co-operation, and the Common Law

JOHN N. HAZARD

JUDGE MANLEY O. HUDSON, when Professor at the Harvard Law School, taught his students that international lawyers could do without knowledge of the law of war. His course centered attention on the emerging elements of international co-operation and especially upon multi-lateral treaties, which in Judge Hudson's view constituted "international legislation." In support of his theory he initiated his noted series of volumes bearing that name.

Hudson was at his best in the 1930's. The Kellogg-Briand Pact of 1928 had prepared the way for his position by out-lawing war as an instrument of national policy. He expected tensions to continue for some time, but war would be avoided because it had become illegal when used to achieve national ends. Its sole remaining place was as a sanction within the framework of the Covenant of the League of Nations.

A basic assumption underlying the strain of thinking in the United States which Hudson represented was that all states of the world were moving slowly but perceptibly towards common social foundations, which would lead ultimately to the unification of law and the emergence of a world community of sorts. The comparative study of law was becoming popular, and the Institute for the Unification of Private Law in Rome was receiving the support of numerous governments who looked to it for leadership towards unity in fundamentals. No one expected the great religions to merge, but since the Thirty Years' War religious peace among Christians had been presumed, and it looked in the 1930's as if religious wars in non-Christian areas were unlikely. There was, however, one small cloud on the horizon. Political ideologies had been shaken in 1917 with the emergence of the Bolsheviks, but Lloyd George had brought Russia back to the concert of Europe at the Genoa Conference of 1922. It was expected to be troublesome for a while, but many suggested that the history of the French Revolution would be repeated and that revolutionary ardour would cool. The Russians, although believed to be not quite the same as other Europeans, were expected to quiet their efforts to revolutionize the world. The Commintern had continued to hold congresses, even into the 1930's, but at less frequent intervals, for since 1924 its light had dimmed with its failure in the Far East to establish a nucleus of revolutionary ardour among the peoples of Asia.

Onto this hopeful scene came Hitler. Informed citizens of the United States saw him as a menace, but most of the citizenry expected to contain him by some means or other. Men like Professor Edwin C. Borchard of Yale urged international lawyers to retreat from Europe and to leave it to settle its own quarrels. Hudson was not easily alarmed, and he continued to omit the law of war from his courses, but others began to question whether world union under law was to be achieved until another world war had so frightened people that they would demand it. The League of Nations was losing its appeal even to those who had hoped for much, for it could do nothing to save Ethiopia or China. War was being used as an instrument of national policy, and it was proving successful. The vision of unity was dim, but for many in the United States it was but postponed. It had not become utopian.

This background is necessary to understand current thinking on the demand heard in many parts of the world today that the aim must be "peaceful co-existence of states of differing social and economic systems." To those who have long anticipated increasing harmony, the premise of peaceful co-existence is discouraging. It suggests that states are not moving in the same direction to ultimate union, but that they will remain in opposing camps from which only conflict can emerge. The most that can be hoped for under such a programme is that conflict will not lead to war. The idea of such a limited goal is distasteful, as evidenced by the large number of authors and of delegates to the United Nations who have raised their voices against use of the term. To accept it seems to many to admit defeat in the age-long struggle to unite mankind in a volunteeristic society.

The communists in the U.S.S.R., China, and the smaller People's Democracies have fed the flames of disillusionment in the West. When the Prime Minister of the U.S.S.R., in January, 1961, said that "peaceful co-existence is a form of intensive economic, political, and ideological struggle," all hope that the history of the French revolution would be repeated within the foreseeable future was dimmed, especially since his willingness to set aside war as an instrument of revolution was disclosed to be based only on fear of destruction of his own country.

To calm those who were alarmed around the world by the Prime Minister's words, Soviet diplomats soon appeared in print and on international platforms to say that peaceful co-existence included not only absence of war but also some

measure of co-operation, but the Communist Party programme for the U.S.S.R., when published in October, 1961,
repeated, "Peaceful co-existence serves as the basis for the
peaceful competition between socialism and capitalism on
an international scale and constitutes a specific form of class
struggle between them." The only saving grace of this plat-
form was the word "peaceful," which was explained by a
sentence in close relationship which read, "War cannot and
must not serve as a means of settling international disputes."

Had peaceful co-existence remained subject solely to
definition by communists of the U.S.S.R., there might have
been many who would have thought it worthwhile to accept
the term for what it was, a renunciation of war, not because
it was morally evil in the sense that the Kellogg-Briand Pact
thought it evil but because it was mutually destructive even
to the point of annihilation of much of mankind. But the
Chinese would not have it so. They had also declared
peaceful co-existence to be the basis of their foreign policy,
for in their 1954 treaty with India over Tibet they made
peaceful co-existence one of the five pillars of policy. The
following year at Bandoeng they had sponsored inclusion
of this term among the guiding principles in relationships of
peoples of Asia and Africa. Then had followed what the
Prime Minister of India has declared to be an aggression
by the Chinese People's Republic against India. And after
that the heads of state of Indonesia, the Philippines, and
Malaya had become concerned to such an extent with
Chinese intentions that they had met in an effort to
arrange some form of mutual defence.

Even the communists of the U.S.S.R. became alarmed,
as the West learned only with publication of an exchange
of letters in July, 1963, but the break seems to have been
initiated in 1957 when Soviet leaders decided not to help
China with development of atomic weapons. The Soviet
letter asserted that China was willing to risk atomic war in

the spread of the communist system. The Soviets said, "What is the position of the leadership of the Communist Party of China? What can the thesis it is propagandizing mean? War cannot be eliminated while imperialism still exists; peaceful co-existence is an illusion, it cannot be the general principle of the foreign policies of the socialist countries; the struggle for peace impedes the revolutionary struggle."

Having established the previously undisclosed nature of the Chinese position, the Soviet communists ask a final question, "We would like to ask the Chinese comrades, who propose building a beautiful future on the ruins of the old world destroyed in thermonuclear war: Have they consulted on this question with the working class in those countries where imperialism reigns?" Then they hurl a final charge that the Chinese seek not class revolution but prevalence of the East wind over the wind from the West, namely the supremacy of China over the world, including the U.S.S.R.

Peaceful co-existence as a goal of foreign policy means different things to different communists, as is evident from the Sino-Soviet exchange. The contrast in communist views is further emphasized when the Yugoslav communists make their speeches. They deny that peaceful co-existence is a policy to be applied only in relations between communist-led states and those where communists have not triumphed, as the Soviet and Chinese communists argue. The Yugoslav communists demand that the principle be applied to relations between communist-led states as well, probably having in mind their own conflict with Stalin when he tried his best to overcome them after the split in 1948. They go further. They ask that the policy of peaceful co-existence be made "active," which they explain to be the equivalent of "co-operation." In short, for Yugoslav communists the foreign policy of communist states must look not only to the absence of war but to the initiation of measures of co-operation for the foreseeable future. Being communists they would not abandon the goal of world-wide acceptance of their way of life, but they are prepared for the moment, at least, to let the world's peoples reach this goal at their own pace and through their own resources.

Polish communists adopt a more discouraged position, drawn probably from their own long experience with the partitions. They reject the utopian vision of the West that ruled the minds of men in the late 1920's and early 1930's. They see no present hope of achieving a world united, and they do not believe that there ever was such a possibility. Co-existence to them has been but the state of world relations when there was no war, and it now epitomizes international relations for all time. It has become permanent, and not just a temporary breathing period. It means the absence of war, since war is now unthinkable with the advent of the atomic bomb. It also means the end of state isolation, since in the modern world no state can remain isolated at its own desire, nor can it be isolated by others. All have to live together without war, and this is "co-existence." There is no need to add "active" as a modifying adjective, as the Yugoslavs would, as co-existence requires activity for its preservation, but this activity cannot be full co-operation in a world of differing economic and social systems, each competing for the minds of men.

Were peaceful co-existence to be in usage only by communists, the democracies of the West might well dismiss it from their concern and let the communists argue among themselves. But the term is popular in circles that are not communist. The intellectuals of Asia and Africa have seized upon it in a different sense. For them, as evidenced in debates within the United Nations, it stands for a new relationship between the former colonial powers and the newly independent states. Even some of the long-established states, and notably Thailand, have expressed their view that revision of international law to bring it into accord with the new relationships of equality of all states not only in formal terms, but in all ways is necessary, while the United Arab Republic has demanded that the law be altered to require the former colonial powers to assist development of the states from which they derived much of their wealth.

Peaceful co-existence becomes under this reading not only a slogan of the communists. It emerges as a catchword summarizing the aspiration of the have-nots. Those who would oppose peaceful co-existence place themselves in the eyes of jurists of the emerging states in the position of the old régime, which was prepared to utilize force to compel weak states to accept interpretation of international law by the strong. Peaceful co-existence becomes a term which would make unlawful the sending of gunboats to threaten the foreign offices of the weak, and would outlaw reprisals against nationalization of foreign investment. Peaceful co-existence means equality with the strong in framing foreign and even domestic policies without fear and with as little thought to what other powers think as the have-nots believe the strong powers give to the thoughts of others in the formulation of their own policies.

What are the sanctions compelling adherence to a policy of peaceful co-existence? For the Soviet spokesmen, it is evident that the primary one is fear of annihilation if the policy is breached. For the Chinese there seems to be no sanction, if Soviet views of Chinese policy are accepted, although the Chinese have retorted to Soviet comments by saying that even they propose to stop expansion short of provoking all-out war. They admit the potency of the balance of terror as a restraint on ardour and they quarrel with their Soviet colleagues only over the point at which the "brink of terror" is to be reached.

For other nations as well the fear of atomic war is clearly the ultimate sanction, and no international lawyer in enthusiasm for his discipline can overlook that fact, but there may also be another sanction. Some feel certain that there is such a sanction, namely world public opinion. It is in the realm of world public opinion that peaceful co-existence probably plays its most compelling role. A glance at that role is a prerequisite to the formulation of Western attitudes towards the subject and its future development in law.

Had a foreign office in a strong state been urged to consider world public opinion before the events of the Suez crisis, and even for some time thereafter, there would have been many who would have rejected the advice. The remarkable development of the present epoch of expansion of membership in the United Nations has been the change in view of the chancelleries of the strong powers on the role of world public opinion. While resolutions of the General Assembly are still rejected by the established powers as a source of law, and properly so under a literal reading of the Charter of the United Nations, an increasing number of representatives of new states find the resolutions compelling proof of the existence of a consensus which is tantamount to law, if not law itself. When the resolution takes the form of a "Declaration" such as that on Human Rights, there are many, even in the West, who argue that it has become an innovator in the law. Proof is adduced from adoption of the principles of the Universal Declaration of Human Rights by many new constitutions, and from reference to it in doctrinal texts as evidence of the state of the world's conscience. With the ever-clearer impossibility of achieving a Covenant on Human Rights, the Declaration remains the ultimate weapon of those who wish to use it, and their zeal is strengthened by realization that no Covenant is to be expected within the foreseeable future.

What should be the position of North Americans of Common Law heritage when voices are raised in favour of a codification of the legal principles of peaceful co-existence? Reference to the Common Law heritage of North Americans is deliberate, because that heritage has some influence upon attitudes towards codification generally. No one can forget the forceful opposition of Oxford's late Professor James L. Brierly within the committee establishing the International Law Commission to codification of international law. He seemed to feel as a Common Lawyer that the codification process stultified development of international law. He thought it a reduction of principles to their lowest common denominator, a form of compromise, and once it was achieved, a base from which no signatory could depart. For him with his knowledge of the growth of the Common Law, a body of principles established in practice tended to evolve in dynamic and desirable fashion. The dissents of one generation became the majority opinion in the next. Common Law judges looked back to precedent, but they also moved forward to interpret precedent in broad fashion to cover situations which were new only because of minute distinctions they were willing to find in facts. In this way the English law had developed, and international law could be expected to prosper if left to follow the same route.

North Americans of English descent tend to share Brierly's views. There is no love for codification in general, although there is increasing willingness to accept it in commercial fields as with the uniform acts which have spread widely in the United States, and also in what might be called the technical fields of the law of international intercourse, particularly that of commerce, but also the law of diplomatic and consular relations, of conservation and of the sea generally.

In contrast many of the diplomats from states of the Romanist tradition distrust a system of law based on practice. They feel that they can never know where they are.

Also they doubt the wisdom of leaving decisions in principle to *ad hoc* situations. They abhor the Common Law judge's reluctance to speak on matters of principle beyond the facts of the case before him. They prefer to call a conference to resolve the principle, thinking that thereafter the details will fall into order with little further dispute.

When this preference for codification, which is traditional because of Romanist influences upon the majority of the states of the United Nations, coincides with the demand of the new states for acceptance of the procedure of resolution of the General Assembly where their votes now account for the majority, pressures for codification and for "declarations" is strong. The question becomes in many minds not whether the statesmen of Common Law background can resist pressures for codification and declarations but whether they can influence the nature of the codes and declarations which seem to be inevitable, given the current structure of the General Assembly.

The history of the Sixth Committee of the General Assembly of the past five years suggests that it is possible to dissociate the necessity of revision of international law to bring it into accord with the aspirations of the developing states from the term "peaceful co-existence," for the General Assembly has instructed its Sixth Committee to work on the problem of "friendly relations and peaceful co-operation among states." To the communist states this is but a synonym for peaceful co-existence, as they continually declare, but the new states of Africa and Asia seem to have grasped the difference. In this they have been aided by events on the Sino-Indian frontier, and by experience of Guinea and the Congo with diplomatic intrigue in domestic affairs by diplomats of the U.S.S.R. It has become evident what peaceful co-existence means as ideological warfare. Not all is being left to a battle of books, as the Soviet Foreign Minister would have the world believe.

What has been achieved in the General Assembly and its Sixth Committee in separating the concept of "peaceful co-existence" from that of revision of international law to bring it into accord with aspirations of new states has not been duplicated in the non-governmental agencies concerned with international law. The International Law Association placed on its agenda in 1956 a study of the juridical aspects of peaceful co-existence before the emotional link with the policy of communist-led states was fully understood by many of the delegates from states outside the group initiating the move. Since adoption of the topic, it has proved to be impossible to change its name to bring it into accord with the title used in the United Nations, for the national branches from the communist-led states have threatened to withdraw from the Association if this should occur. Faced with a movement that would defeat one of the purposes of a non-governmental agency in which universality is desirable to assure wide discussion and possible compromise of differing positions, the Executive Council of the International Law Association has retained the term and ordered that a list of the principles or rules of peaceful co-existence be completed by August, 1964.

Within the International Association of Democratic Lawyers a similarly directed campaign has led to the placing of peaceful co-existence on its agenda. In this agency, in which delegates from the communist-led powers dominate policy making, there has been even less opportunity than in the International Law Association for opposition-minded delegates even to raise the issue of a change in name of the study.

Thus, in the non-governmental agencies the juridical aspects of peaceful co-existence remain under study, while in the United Nations the emphasis is more clearly upon a concept which is designed not to meet the needs of a communist-oriented foreign policy but of a world in which the developing states are to be accommodated as equal partners with their former masters.

In both the United Nations and the non-governmental agencies concerned with the development of international law the policy of Western-oriented lawyers from the established states is becoming clarified. It is to lead thinking on the subject, whether it be called "peaceful co-existence" or "peaceful co-operation," in the direction of finding a position in international law that will conserve the bulk of the international law that has made for co-operation and peace in the past while introducing those elements of revision that can meet the aspirations of Africans and Asians to be treated equally and in recognition of the dignity that is rightfully theirs.

If seen in this light the task of international lawyers both in and out of governments is to work for solutions in subject after subject of international law which can be satisfying to a majority comprising both lawyers from the established countries and from the developing countries. The United Nations has embarked upon such a process with its resolution of 1963, authorizing the creation of a new commission formed in much the same manner as the International Law Commission but with a more flexible mandate. It is to be concerned with politically desirable solutions and less with codification of existing law. In short, its emphasis is to propose solutions for study in development of the law.

Such a restricted programme will not meet the desires of the communist-led states, for it looks to co-operation of former masters with former colonials, rather than intensification of ideological conflict and expansion of Marxist-type societies, yet the communist-led states cannot oppose it in principle without abdicating their self-proclaimed role as champions of the developing states. They will have to accept the idea. In the United Nations, where votes are by states, they cannot expect to outvote delegates from the rest of the world. Yet, in the International Law Association, where voting is by individuals in attendance at Congresses, an opportunity to outvote non-communists might be presented if the meetings were to be held in a communist-led state, or in a place to which large numbers of delegates from the East European states might be sent. Up to the present there has been no move that could lead to a conclusion that such a strategy is being formulated.

Far more difficult than the arrangement of the machinery for revision of international law along the lines indicated is the determination of what issues require resolution. The Africans have not yet done much in the United Nations to clarify their views, beyond expressing their desire for revision in the interest of recognition of their human dignity. Very few states have seized the opportunity offered in the United Nations by resolution 1815 (XVII) of 18 December, 1962, to forward to the Secretary General views on the items placed on the agenda for study as elements of the law of peaceful co-operation. Yet, there have been developments in the African Continent which require examination, such as creation of the Charter of the Organization for United Africa, signed at Addis Abbaba in 1963, which brings together states of quite different political, social, and economic systems in the vision of an inter-African organization. In this document, as the Belgian delegate to the Sixth Committee suggested in 1963, lies a clue as to the extent to which Africans are willing to reduce the absolute sovereignty of states in the interest of co-operation. The Africans have also, in the first session of the Council of African Ministers held in Dakar in 1963, elaborated a system of mediation, conciliation, and arbitration under their Charter in contrast to the continuing preference of the communist-led countries for diplomatic negotiation of a bi-lateral character over differences.

One tendency of some of the states seeking revision of

international law should be resisted. It is the limitation of international law to the "law of the Charter of the United Nations." Such a limitation suggests that nothing of the international law accepted before 1945 has validity for the postwar world. It is true that there have been extensive developments since 1945 in application of the principles of the Charter which might well be examined and systematized in study of the principles of peaceful co-operation, but this is not to say that all prior practice is impertinent. The falsity of such a view is proved by the Vienna conferences on diplomatic and consular law and the Geneva conferences on the law of the sea. In seeking to establish conventions which will facilitate understanding of the law in these fields, the delegates at these conferences reviewed the practice of the nineteenth century to determine its continuing applicability. No one began with 1945.

Even the Common-Law-oriented states accepted the concept of codification represented by the Vienna and Geneva accords, although both subjects had traditionally been considered essentially based on custom. Under proper safeguards, such as provisions for reconvening of the conference periodically to review desirable amendments, it is possible that Common Law prejudices against codification can be overcome, although the failure of the United Nations to reconvene for Charter revision in spite of provisions anticipating such reviews gives reason to doubt the efficacy of such provisions in keeping a code abreast of practical necessity.

On balance, with primary consideration given to the fact that the majority of the countries of the world are new and their foreign offices are not yet staffed with men trained in international law, as evidenced by requests for technical assistance filed with the United Nations in 1963 in response to resolution 1816 (XVII), the desirability at this stage of efforts to codify international law seems clear. The advantages of a known minimum outweigh the disadvantages of an unknown base, and the Common-Law-oriented states would be wise to take this into consideration, the more so since their colleagues from the Romanist-oriented legal systems of long tradition have no fear that codification prevents evolution.

What then can be concluded? The exigencies of a world where a majority of states are new and uneasy about the present situation in international law which they do not fully understand require efforts to determine what the law is and the direction in which it should move to meet legitimate aspirations for recognition of the dignity of the new states and their peoples. These efforts should as a minimum take the form of study conferences, and since such study is facilitated by consideration of draft conventions which the Romanist-oriented lawyers who will attend understand, they might well be organized as discussions of draft conventions rather than of "restatements," which have come for the Common-Law world to be the alternative. It can be expected that as a result a framework of rules and principles will be established which will look towards increasing co-operation on a world basis, as has come to be the case following similar efforts on a regional basis of recent years. "Peaceful co-existence" as a narrow concept of peace prior to the triumph of the Marxist-oriented social, political, and economic system will become transformed into an identifiable form of peaceful co-operation, and there will no longer be a need to combat its use as an expression denoting the goal of international law.

Objectives and Method in International Law and the East-West *Détente*

EDWARD McWHINNEY

THE SOVIET JURIDICAL CONCEPT of "peaceful co-existence," in spite of the appropriately reverential footnotes to Lenin's assorted writings which contemporary Soviet leaders have sought retrospectively to establish, is essentially a product of the de-Stalinization period in Soviet political life. Like very many Soviet special political-juridical concepts, it has had, in its early origins in the Khrushchev era, a certain inbuilt quality of ambivalence, having seemed sometimes to be merely a convenient propaganda device to baffle and confuse Western leaders while Soviet leaders prepared (in Premier Khrushchev's own very striking phrase) to "bury the West"; and sometimes to reflect a more deep-seated Soviet desire—reacting realistically to the physical facts of life of the nuclear age and the sheer impossibility of either East's or West's rationally contemplating a nuclear war between each other—to accept the political facts of life of the present-day World Community and the apparent *status quo* of the division of the world into the two great contending ideological and power blocs, each with its own more or less clearly defined and mutually recognized or tacitly accepted sphere of political and military influence. This seemingly conscious ambivalence in the term "peaceful co-existence," for Soviet policy-makers and their political advisers and jurists, at least in their public statements and pronouncements, has tended to remain; except that the emphasis and weighting has appeared perceptibly and increasingly to shift away from the neo-Stalinist interpretation towards the policy of what might be called "live-and-let-live" with the West.

Now, we in the West have never, ourselves, at least for any appreciable length of time, had any overly rigid or monolithic conception of what is desirable foreign policy vis-à-vis the Soviet Union and the Soviet bloc generally, but have always sensibly maintained our options on alternative policy constructs, with the actual choice between these constructs turning at any time on the concrete, working facts of international power relations. The Janus-like quality of Soviet policy-makers, in the Khrushchev era of peaceful co-existence, of seeming to try to face both ways at once, should therefore be no real surprise to us; nor should it necessarily present unusual problems for our own foreign ministries of elaborating and projecting ahead the trends in Soviet foreign policy and thus of predicting the responses of Soviet policy-makers to future tension situations of East-West relations. Granting, as Western policy-makers now fairly generally seem to do, that, in the Soviet Union (in marked contrast to Hitler's *Reich*), rational decision-making processes operate in the formulation and implementation of foreign policy, the objective facts of international relations in the nuclear age tend to produce, in the Soviet foreign ministry not less than in Western foreign ministries, eminently foreseeable and calculable, and (from the particular viewpoint of each power bloc) rational, responses in policy terms.

The shift in the Soviet foreign ministry decisively away from the hard line, essentially neo-Stalinist policy construct on peaceful co-existence to what might be called the more moderate approach that, publicly at least, has seemed to stress accommodation with the West, appears to date from the peaceful resolution of the October, 1962, Soviet-Western crisis over the emplacement of Soviet offensive, ground-to-ground, nuclear missiles in Cuba. Although in the face of the resolute response for the West by President Kennedy, Premier Khrushchev did in fact withdraw his offensive, ground-to-ground, nuclear missiles from Cuba, he nevertheless did so, as Walter Lippmann has rightly noted, gracefully, even elegantly; and President Kennedy's own actions in response to this were characterized, for his part, by a conscious moderation and restraint, both of action and utterance. The lesser, indirect means, pacific blockade, was used as the inducement to the Soviet Union to withdraw its offensive, ground-to-ground, nuclear missiles from Cuba; where some more overt and direct Western action, such as actually bombing the Cuban offensive nuclear missile bases, might have compelled the Soviet Union, if only to avoid intolerable loss of face, to stand its ground, with a resultant imminent risk of escalation of the crisis into general, nuclear war. The means of control employed by President Kennedy were sufficient, and no more than sufficient, to remove the clear and present danger actually encountered; and when Premier Khrushchev did in fact finally withdraw, President Kennedy noticeably refrained from elaborate victory claims. The actual *modus operandi* for peacefully resolving the October, 1962, crisis, probably is what finally served to persuade the key Soviet and Western leaders of the necessary minimum element of responsibility in decision-making, on both sides, without which of course no East-West agreement or accommodation in any sense could pretend to be viable. The successful achievement by the Soviet Union, the United States, and Great Britain, in August,

1963, of the Moscow Partial Test Ban Treaty and the subsequent Soviet-United States agreement in the United Nations to prevent the orbiting of nuclear weapons in outer space, on this interpretation, would simply confirm and extend, in the sense of rendering more concrete, explicit, and definite, a substantive accommodation, involving fundamentals, already recognized *de facto* by the Soviet Union and the West, in the peaceful resolution of the October, 1962, crisis.

For the international lawyer called on to advise in the practical effectuation of any East-West *détente*, certain important questions of legal method remain with regard to the choice of the appropriate means or instruments for the reduction of East-West tensions generally and also to the choice of arenas for East-West confrontation with a view to any such settlements. We must here distinguish, I think, between what might be called, not inappropriately, the *polemics* of the competition of the two main opposing legal systems, Soviet and Western, and the more sober, usually only half-articulated, positions actually taken by Soviet and Western policy-makers in their face-to-face dealings. Thus Soviet international lawyers uniformly denigrate "custom," in the sense of historically developed and recognized rules of practice between states, as a source of international law; and have gone so far as to contend that only where a rule of custom is expressly accepted by any state will it be binding, as law, upon that state at the present day. The attractiveness of theories such as these to newly independent countries, or to older countries which have in modern times undergone major political, economic, or social revolutions, are obvious, just as is the clear Soviet preference for bilateral treaties as the prime source of international law at the present day. For the preference for the bilateral treaty as a source of international law gives priority of emphasis also to the voluntaristic element in international law—that is, the notion that the principles of international law, if they are to be binding on states, must truly be the product of the consent or agreement of states; where the emphasis on custom, by contrast, has occasionally seemed to be redolent of a bygone, almost "mediæval," status era in international relations in which states, so to speak, entered a political system that they were powerless to change. Part of this apparent dead-hand control aspect of historical custom is no doubt the fault of Western scholars who have too often in the past seemed to be attempting unimaginatively and literally to apply old custom to control present-day events and forces. The lack of attraction of any such theories for dynamic or revolutionary societies today is patent. But, beyond that, the Soviet emphasis on bilateral treaties as the prime source of international law today seems very well attuned to the factual, existential condition of the present World Community of the division into the two great contending power blocs, together with the acceptance by both sides, for quite practical reasons in a nuclear age, of the impossibility of changing that basic condition by direct, military means. This both results in a certain parity of bargaining power between each side, and also ensures that any agreement or accommodation reached between them will be a genuine *quid pro quo* or bargain, involving bilateralism and reciprocity and mutual give-and-take. The bilateral treaty, preferably achieved through a Summit Meeting *à deux* between the two bloc leaders, seems indeed to be not merely the preferred instrument of Soviet and Western policy-makers for the achievement of East-West substantive accommodations in the present era, but also to be the most logical and rational means of achieving viable accommodations, granted the present power realities in the World Community.

The Western legal response to Soviet legal initiative in furtherance of the Soviet campaign in behalf of peaceful co-existence has frequently seemed to be rather negative and defensive. We have failed to develop an adequately institutionally-based theory as to the necessary relation between law and social change, paralleling, in the international sphere, the dynamic theories for the progressive development and re-shaping of the positive law which have become so influential in Western legal science in the internal or municipal sphere under the impetus of the pragmatist-realist impulse in Western legal philosophy. We have, as already noted, tended to stress the conservative element in customary international law, failing always to appreciate that the life-force of custom, as the major source through time of the present-day *corpus* of international law rules, has been its inbuilt dynamic quality or stress on historical continuity in the *development* and *unfolding* of those rules, and not any necessary acceptance of the *status quo* and stand-pat, literal application of old rules in new fact-situations. Likewise, in tending to reject all the pressures to use direct bargains and agreements—bilateral treaties—as agencies for the rewriting, on an equitable basis, of time-worn old rules, we have perhaps, in the West, too mechanically invoked the recourse to the United Nations and to specialized institutions like the World Court, as useful arenas for new international law-making. The Soviet bloc has, over the years, been so consistently outvoted or out-manoeuvred by the West in the United Nations and its specialized agencies, as to feel, with some occasional justice perhaps, that the West is proffering the suggestions for recourse to the United Nations and equally to the World Court only for reasons of tactical advantage and of the assumed continuance of pro-Western voting majorities in these bodies. The West, for its own part—though U.S. Secretary of State Dean Rusk's Dag Hammarskjold Address at Columbia University on January 10, 1964, in sounding a first official, United States note of mild scepticism as to the United Nations' full contemporary usefulness for contemporary problem-solving in international relations, may well herald a change—has failed to give satisfactory attention to the need for strengthening the United Nations machinery, to ensure some greater degree of responsiveness between the increasingly unstable and capricious General Assembly majority coalitions of forces, and the elemental facts of life as to the burden of power and responsibility of the great powers in the contemporary World Community. And even as to the World Court, some of the currently professed Western positions in support of a widespread extension of its present jurisdiction may sound rather hollow in the absence of any concomitant Western pressure for strengthening of the intellectual calibre and representativeness of that body through an elimination of at least the more overt elements of political horse-trading and casual patronage that have marked some of the Western and Soviet bloc sponsorships of candidates for election as judges of the Court in the postwar years.

Fortunately for prospects of East-West accommodation at the present time, the seeming absolutism of the rival East-West doctrinal positions, as represented in attitudes such as these, are considerably modified in the actual practice of East-West relations. The Soviet Union, perhaps influenced by the fact that, as successor government to the old pre-1917 Tsarist government of Russia, it is the beneficiary, in terms of international law, of the quite considerable benefits inhering in Russia under customary international law and under "old" treaties—not least perhaps in relation to Russia's present-day territorial frontiers with Communist China, whose title stems essentially from mid-nineteenth century agreements supplemented by custom— concedes in practice that not all "old" custom is bad *per se* and therefore to be rejected out-of-hand as a source of binding international law rules at the present day. The West is finding itself sufficiently irritated with what it considers the frequent irrationality or irresponsibility of the U.N. General Assembly majorities of recent years to look increasingly, in practice, to what a high U.S. official calls "alternative peace-keeping institutions," and to try to transact the really important business of East-West relations, and therefore of World peace generally, away from the hurly-burly and the all too frequent posturing and "playing to the galleries" attendant on any negotiations or similar transactions at the United Nations itself. Actually, the current preference on both sides, East and West, for quiet diplomacy, quietly applied to the quest for limited but concrete agreements, worked out jointly by the bloc leaders on each side and only subsequently presented by them to third parties for their adherence and without any power on the part of those third parties to change or modify the substantive provisions of the agreement, seems to have led the West quietly to accept the Soviet Union's pressure for recourse to the bilateral treaty as the main instrument for East-West fundamental accommodations. On this basis, as the common East-West operational methodology for achievement of the partial ban on nuclear testing—through the Moscow Partial Test Ban Treaty of August, 1963—seems to indicate, the bilateral treaty is likely to become the prime source of at least the new international law of East-West relations of this present, nuclear era.

Going beyond questions of formal sources of international law and arenas for international law-making in general, however, there are still certain important questions as to basic legal method and legal philosophy, as between the two great contending legal systems, which seem important to any fundamental East-West accommodation. I am aware that it is sometimes considered good juristic gamesmanship, in the West, to score points off Soviet jurists by quoting old definitions of law from the Stalinist era—usually Vyshinsky's highly positivistic, neo-Austinian, "command" definition—as evidence that Soviet law in general, and therefore Soviet international law in particular, must be highly autocratic or dictatorial, and that it is, therefore, by definition, illiberal, in contrast to classical, Western-based international law; or again to quote latter-day, more instrumentalist Soviet definitions of law, to emphasize that international law, for the Soviet Union, is a simple veil for masking policy exercises that stem from considerations of naked power alone. Both these types of criticism ignore, I believe, the changing character of Soviet international legal science, especially in the most recent, Khrushchev era, and also the extent to which, in fact, more pragmatist, problem-solving methods have taken over among the younger members of the Soviet legal "establishment," especially those grouped around Professor Tunkin, the present Principal Legal Adviser to the Soviet Foreign Ministry. This trend in the Soviet legal establishment over the last decade parallels the dominant emphasis in North American law schools in the postwar years under the influence of pragmatist-realist ideas in general legal philosophy, and ultimately (since the younger governmental policy-makers are so largely the products, themselves, of this very impulse in the law schools) the dominant emphasis in the State Department itself and some other Western foreign ministries. In any case, the call, in postwar North American legal education, for more imaginative and flexible, policy-oriented approaches to old legal doctrine and also for frank utilization of social science techniques—sociological jurisprudence—as an aid in legal problem-solving, is such as to render the conventional, rather tired, pejorative remarks and clichés about the "arbitrary," "instrumental" character of Soviet legal science not very helpful or operationally useful in the approach to the legal accommodation of East-West conflicts. Actually, it is the current rather pragmatic, problem-solving approach that is noticeable in the best of the younger Soviet jurists that opens up such fruitful possibilities for genuinely viable East-West accommodations; for the basic legal method approaches our own dominant legal method sufficiently to make serious scientific discussion between our two opposing legal systems for the first time really meaningful.

Related to this question is the problem, too often forgotten, that Soviet law is not merely Socialist but also, in its received historical tradition and its basic procedures and institutions and even, in certain areas, in its substantive principles, in measure Romanist and Civil Law. Professor Hazard has suggested, in his excellent essay in this volume, that the West should defer to this received Romanist or Civil Law element in Soviet law by yielding to the current Soviet predilection, as expressed in the continuing Soviet pressure in the United Nations Sixth Committee, in the International Law Commission of the United Nations, and also in the authoritative (though professional and scientific, and non-governmental), International Law Association, for an immediate codification of the principles of peaceful co-existence. I should be sorry if, in our present very commendable readiness to abandon our past, and occasionally rather objectionable, manifestations of purely Anglo-Saxon Common Law legal nationalism, we should give way on this point which seems to me to be fundamental.

So far as it is contended that the Continental European Civil Lawyers prefer abstract general declarations of the nature of the Kellogg-Briand Pact of 1928 to more concrete, low-level, modest agreements, it seems to me that there is little in those Continental European Civil Lawyers' record to inspire confidence as to a viability of their basic, preferred method in terms of any attempted fundamental East-West accommodations. The Continental European Civil Lawyers of the era between the two world wars seem frankly to have enjoyed the poetry involved in drafting high-sounding declarations of abstract general principle, perhaps because it immunized them from the tiresome responsibility of dealing with the dynamics of power involved in translating any such agreements into working reality. The legal *honoratiores* (to use Max Weber's term) of Continental Europe of the between-the-two-wars era may, in this sense, bear a heavy personal responsibility for having deluded or disappointed people with their all-exclusive preoccupation with the purely chimerical or fanciful in *de facto* legal relationships between states. Some of General de Gaulle's contemporary pragmatic empiricism, as distinct of course from his grandeur, may sorely have been needed by the French, and by Continental European civil lawyers generally, in their approach to international law between the two wars.

More important, in the present context of East-West relationships, further attempts at codification of abstract general principles are likely to be so very vague as to be meaningless in action, in terms of the attempted resolution (on a basis mutually acceptable to East and West, and mutually capable, therefore, of ascertainment and determination in advance of the actual problem) of actual problems of East-West tension. There is thus a real danger that any such attempts at codification will be purely rhetorical or hortatory, exercises in natural-law–type affirmations, with the practical disadvantage that Western-based natural law and natural law Marxist-style may have rather different philosophical premises, yielding rather different solutions in actual cases when the abstract, high-level, primary declarations of a code are sought to be rendered explicit and operational in terms of more concrete secondary principles. There may be a place, to be sure, in the polemics of East-West legal competition for trading verbal blows in terms of such high-level, and (operationally) immediately unusable abstractions as the Soviet-sponsored "Socialist International Law," and the Western, private pressure-group–sponsored counter-concept of a "World Rule of Law," but neither seems to be really helpful in the sober and serious business of attempting fundamental East-West accommodations.

At the fiftieth jubilee reunion of the International Law Association, held in Brussels in August, 1962—when the Cold War was still on, two months, indeed, before the last great Soviet-Western confrontation, over the Soviet offensive nuclear missiles in Cuba—Western jurists said, in effect, to Soviet jurists: Be concrete, be specific! Let us take actual problems of East-West relations; let us study them calmly and soberly; let us see if there are not common solutions to these problems, based on remedies that would be mutually advantageous to both the Soviet Union and the West. If we find any such common—reciprocally beneficial, in East-West terms—solutions to any such problems, then we can make a viable agreement, meaning one that rests not on windy rhetoric alone but on tangible prospects of being maintained equally by East and West because of the mutual give-and-take involved in the agreement itself.

Here was the genesis of a step-by-step, problem-oriented approach to East-West relations, which had its most striking vindication, after the peaceful resolution of the October, 1962, East-West crisis (a crisis, again, resolved not in terms of absolute and total victory on either side, but on a basis of reciprocity and mutual exchange) in the operational method used by both East and West for achievement of the Moscow Partial Test Ban Treaty of August, 1963. This method is, of course, essentially low-level, empirically-based. It will not please those on either side who want the Sermon on the Mount or a Holy War against the other side. But it has enabled both sides, sitting down for negotiation in an atmosphere refreshingly free from Cold War propaganda and rhetoric, to explore, in a calm and scientific spirit, the possibility of further common solutions to common problems of East and West. It is in this very spirit that President Johnson, responding on January 20, 1964, to Premier Khrushchev's very encouraging, year's end letter, 1963, to the Heads of State, has asked Mr. Khrushchev to continue in the spirit of the Moscow Partial Test Ban Treaty and therefore to accept that the main task, today, is: "to work hard and persistently . . . on specific problems and proposals —as you and President Kennedy did on the Test Ban Treaty—instead of confining ourselves to vague declarations of principle."

There is every reason to believe that if the new spirit of pragmatism can be continued and accepted on both sides and translated into further specific agreements, based on mutual, East-West give-and-take, then the present East-West *détente*, finding, as it does, its *raison d'être* in certain objective facts of the World Community in the nuclear age and, above all, the clear impossibility of either East's or West's rationally contemplating a nuclear war as an instrument of national policy, can be really translated, in time, from a limited accommodation or truce into some more genuinely comprehensive and universal international law of human dignity.

Co-existence or
Friendly Relations?
The Canadian Approach

THE HON. PAUL MARTIN

I AM PLEASED to have this opportunity to comment briefly on certain topical questions of international law, and I shall try to explain how we endeavour to implement Canadian policy on these questions through Canadian diplomacy in the U.N.

In an address I delivered to the Montreal Section of the Canadian Branch of the International Law Association in Montreal on October 2, 1963, I dealt in some detail with various Soviet theories of international law, in particular the Soviet approach to "peaceful co-existence," both as a political and a legal concept. I attempted to explain in that address why the Soviet concept of co-existence falls short of the minimal needs of the world community as a basis of friendly relations and co-operation among states. It will be recalled too that I stressed that the term co-existence may represent to many non-communist states, particularly some of the less-developed countries who have espoused the doctrine, something totally different from what it means to communist countries. I pointed out that throughout the debates in the U.N. concerning the feasibility and utility of attempting to codify the "principles of co-existence," Canada has attempted to play a constructive role and to avoid espousing positions which, however sound under existing international law, may not be sufficiently responsive to the desires of the new states to have a hand in the shaping of the kind of world order in which they wish to live. In outlining some aspects of the Canadian approach to this question I hope to illustrate what I meant by these remarks.

Before discussing Canadian diplomacy in the U.N. concerning the co-existence debate, I should refer briefly to the continuing discussions of the International Law Association concerning the codification of co-existence. Because of the highly political nature of the subject, a number of governments, including that of Canada, are watching these discussions with interest. The International Law Association is a non-governmental organization, however (composed, I believe, of some 3,000 or more practitioners and professors of international law), and over the years, we in Canada have been conscious of the need to maintain the independence of the Canadian Branch of the I.L.A. As a consequence we have not, for instance, ever sent an official delegation to the biennial conferences of the organization, although legal officers from the Department of External Affairs, and occasionally from other Canadian government departments, have attended nearly every one of the biennial conferences in recent years, as observers. Such officers have been briefed on the subjects being studied and have been available for discussions and consultation with other members of the Canadian Branch, but have not intervened in the debates of the Association. Two of our officers were present, for instance, at the last conference in Brussels when the debate as to the utility of attempting to codify the "principles of co-existence" took place. We have been aware, of course, that other countries less mindful of the need, or, indeed, the possibility (in the cases of Soviet bloc countries) of maintaining the distinction between official-dom and private citizens, have been sending what has amounted to official delegations to the Conferences. We know too that the representatives of these countries, often the same officials who have attended the I.L.A. meetings, have subsequently quoted their own self-serving evidence in various organs of the U.N. as proof of the validity of their arguments. Western countries have preferred to leave it to the integrity and competence of their respective branches to contend with these developments, and this has been and will continue to be the Canadian approach. We remain, of course, ready and willing to provide information and consult, to the extent considered desirable by the Canadian Branch, concerning the questions being studied. I should like to emphasize, however, the desirability of bearing in mind that the International Law Association is a non-governmental organization and that its decisions cannot carry with it the sanction and approval of the governments from whose countries its members may be drawn. This, I believe, is as the members of the I.L.A. would have it, and this characteristic of the organization, I would suggest, should be maintained at all cost, if the Association is to continue to play a useful role in the study and development of international law.

Turning to the activities within the U.N. concerning the co-existence question, the two bodies within which the question is in issue in one form or another are the International Law Commission and the Sixth Committee of the United Nations. The International Law Commission, it will be recalled, was established by the General Assembly in 1947 as a body of independent legal experts to promote the codification and progressive development of international law. The Commission has recently been increased to a membership of twenty-five jurists, selected on the basis of their personal legal competence and as representing the principal legal systems and geographical areas of the world; the members of the Commission are not representatives of their respective governments, although in some cases officials of various countries are members of the International Law Commission by virtue of their personal eminence in the field of international law. Canada, for instance, is fortunate in having Mr. Marcel Cadieux, Deputy Under-Secretary of State for External Affairs and Legal Adviser to the Department, as a member of the Commission. Mr. Cadieux is, of course, in a unique position to bring to bear a knowledge of both the Common and civil law traditions of Canada, and as our Legal Adviser he is a practising international lawyer as well as a professor of law associated with Ottawa University.

The International Law Commission is not concerned with the codification of the principles of co-existence. Nonetheless, one of the subjects now being studied, namely "state responsibility," has provided opportunities for proponents of the Soviet version of co-existence to introduce the well-known arguments on the question into the deliberations of the International Law Commission. The I.L.C. is, because of its nature and composition, able to take what I would term a more legal than political approach to such questions. It should be kept in mind, however, that what goes on in the International Law Association and in the Sixth Committee of the U.N., to which I shall refer in a moment, can have implications for the important work of the International Law Commission, which is the U.N. organ seized with the specific task of promoting the progressive development and codification of international law.

Turning now to the Sixth Committee, I do not propose to canvass the history within that Committee of the various attempts to have a study made of the "principles of co-existence." It will be recalled that an item entitled "Friendly relations and co-operation among states in accordance with the Charter of the U.N." was placed on the agenda of the Sixth Committee during the Sixteenth Session of the U.N. after considerable debate concerning the title of the item. Subsequently, in the Seventeenth Session of the U.N., a resolution was tabled by Canada and other like-minded countries calling for an affirmation of the rule of law amongst nations and of the United Nations Charter as the fundamental statement of principles underlying friendly relations, and for a study of two areas of the law in need of clarification and development (the principle of respect for the territorial integrity and political independence of states and the obligation to settle disputes by peaceful means). Two other resolutions were introduced on the same item, one by Czechoslovakia and the other by Yugoslavia and a number of other countries, both calling for a declaration of principles which should govern friendly relations among states.

The Canadian Delegation subsequently carried the main burden of negotiating a compromise with the co-sponsors of the two other resolutions. The resulting resolution* stressed the importance of the continuing development of the rule of law among nations and the Charter as the fundamental statement of principles of international law governing friendly relations and co-operation among states (as listed in the resolution), and concluded with the decision to commence a study of the two principles contained in the Canadian-sponsored resolution, plus two further principles (those of "non-intervention" and "sovereign equality of states") suggested by other delegations. This resolution was approved unanimously by the General Assembly. I think it may be appropriate to explain at this point how it came about that Canada has played such an active role on this question.

*Resolution No. 1815 (XVII).

Some time ago it became apparent, during the course of various studies made within the Department of External Affairs, that there was cause for concern over some relatively recent trends which showed signs of being inimical to the future development of international law along orderly lines. These tendencies emanated chiefly, in our view, from the direct attacks being made by the Soviet bloc upon many of the established bases of international law. Not surprisingly, some non-communist countries, aware of the importance of maintaining the structure of law within which international affairs are conducted, responded unsympathetically to demands for a "new international law," with the result that it sometimes appeared that the Soviet bloc was more sensitive than non-communist nations to the legitimate aspirations of the newer nations of the world (the majority of whom are of course themselves firmly non-communist). There was, in other words, a situation developing in which Western nations in particular were sometimes obliged to attack concepts they could not accept, without having the opportunity to demonstrate the validity of those fundamental principles of law whose importance has been established over the years. What kind of response should be made, for instance, to a demand for codification of such soundly based principles as self-determination, sovereign equality, non-intervention, and sovereignty, without accepting the restrictive and regressive interpretation of such principles given to them by communist countries in subsuming them under the rubric of "peaceful co-existence"? It was time, in our view, that the non-communist countries of the world began to cease merely reacting to questionable initiatives and to take the lead in making constructive proposals specifically designed to broaden the legal base of the mutuality of interests which clearly exists, in spite of the differences of which we hear so much, between Western and non-aligned countries, and even between Western and communist countries.

With these considerations in mind, we instructed our diplomats in various capitals to raise these questions with a view to stimulating greater interest in them, in the hopes of eventually developing a broadly based initiative designed to meet some of the practical needs of the community of nations in the field of international law. The next step in the process occurred in the opening weeks of the Seventeenth Session of the United Nations, when members of the Canadian Delegation sat down with members of other delegations to draft a resolution aimed at embodying and implementing the ideas and proposals which had been developed as a result of our discussions with other countries. I am not sure whether it is generally known that this stage of drafting is one of the most important in the launching of any initiative in the U.N. The next step was to ascertain whether the resulting draft resolution had any chance of receiving broad support within the U.N. Copies of the resolution were therefore shown to other friendly delegations (not merely to the Western, of course, but also to some of the important non-aligned nations). Certain doubts and reservations were expressed concerning some aspects of the resolution, and some changes were made as a result. The next step was to seek out a group of co-sponsors which would be broadly based, but would nonetheless have a strong mutuality of interests in the proposals embodied in the resolution, since otherwise the inevitable pressures which would arise would result in the loss of certain key co-sponsors. A whole series of meetings was held with other delegations, culminating in the tabling of a draft resolution co-sponsored by Canada, the Cameroons, Chile, Columbia, Dahomey, Denmark, Japan, Liberia, Nigeria, Pakistan, the Philippines, Sierra Leone, and Tanganyika. It will be noted that this group included an interesting cross-section of member states of the U.N.—one of the prerequisites to achieving general support for a proposal. Throughout the

debate on the friendly relations item these co-sponsors outlined the arguments in favour of their proposal, each one
stressing a different aspect of the concepts embodied in the
resolution. The resolution attracted wide interest and support in the Sixth Committee, and seemed assured of a
sizable majority. Meanwhile, however, a resolution sponsored by Yugoslavia, Afghanistan, Algeria, Cambodia,
Ceylon, Ethiopia, Ghana, India, Indonesia, Mali, Morocco,
Somalia, Syria, and the United Arab Republic, was attract-
ing support, and a resolution sponsored by Czechoslovakia
was also obtaining some support, limited chiefly to the
Soviet bloc.

The difference between the three resolutions might be
summarized as follows: whereas what became known as the
Canadian resolution advocated a study of specific areas of
the law in need of development and clarification, the other
two resolutions called for a declaration or code of principles
of international law. The differences between the Yugoslav
resolution, as it became known, and the Czech resolution
was that the former, while including a number of principles
which, in the view of many U.N. member states, were not
wholly compatible with the principles of the Charter, nevertheless represented an attempt to put forth a number of
generally acceptable principles; the Czech resolution, on the
other hand, simply outlined the Soviet view of international
affairs, and contained a mixture of legal principles, alleged
legal principles, and expressions of political viewpoints.

Great pressure arose within the Committee for some
attempt to work out a compromise between the three resolutions. The result was that the Czech, the Yugoslav, and the
Canadian delegations were named to carry out this task.
For two weeks the representatives of the three countries
met in the office of the Legal Counsel for the U.N., who
sat in throughout the discussions. Every phrase, indeed in
some cases every word of certain phrases, was debated and

discussed. An interesting aspect of the question is that the Canadian Delegation had the task of representing not only the views of the co-sponsors of the resolution with which Canada was associated, but also, by agreement, the views of Western nations who were not co-sponsors of any of the three resolutions. (This is a position in which Canadian diplomats not infrequently find themselves. While sharing a wide range of interests with other Western nations—and it would be dishonest to pretend that we do not—we also habitually, almost instinctively, find ourselves also sharing, and, on occasion, representing, the points of view of other nations.)

The result of the negotiations was the resolution previously referred to. Like all compromises it contained elements reflecting the points of view of all parties to the negotiations; like all compromises—all successful ones that is—it represented no one point of view to the total exclusion of any other; like all compromises it contained imperfections which would be missing from a clear-cut proposal setting forth a single approach. This is the resolution which the Sixth Committee of the U.N. will be using as its basis of operations on the friendly relations question for several years to come.

My reason for explaining in such detail how the resolution came into being is, firstly, to show the nature and extent of the interest Canada has shown in these questions, and secondly, to explain something of Canadian diplomacy in action on questions of international law. Obviously, these questions can never be treated as strictly legal in nature. On the other hand, we have attempted to maintain an essentially legal approach as much as possible, to eschew cold war polemics, and to dissuade others from indulging in them, in the hopes of gradually building a basis of accommodation between differing and sometimes opposing concepts.

In the Eighteenth Session of the U.N., in the fall of 1963,

once again, just as in the preceding year, more than one-half of the meetings of the Session were devoted to this item.

In accordance with the resolution previously referred to, the group of principles of international law concerning friendly relations and co-operation among states was given preliminary examination by the Sixth Committee. Comments which had already been received from various governments, including the Canadian government, and the brisk debate during the Session, evinced many shades of opinion and some fundamental differences of view concerning the manner in which and the extent to which these Charter principles have been reflected in the practice of states and of the United Nations over the last eighteen years. There was as a consequence sharp disagreement over the need to reformulate all or any of these principles. Ideological considerations threatened during a good part of the Session to disrupt the debate, but eventually a resolution was unanimously agreed to, setting up a Special Sub-Committee of the Sixth Committee to meet before the Nineteenth Session and prepare recommendations as to what form the further treatment of each principle should take.

The Canadian Delegation once again took an active part in this discussion, stressing the desirability of avoiding the introduction of highly political considerations into an already difficult legal debate, and it was able to assist in bringing about the compromise resolution. Canada also co-sponsored, as part of its approach to the peaceful settlement of disputes, a resolution initiated by the Netherlands Delegation calling for a study of methods of international fact-finding. This resolution was adopted by 65 (Canada) in favour, 15 (Soviet bloc and some others) against, with 27 abstentions.

I would commend to all serious students of international law the examination of the written comments of member states of the U.N. submitted on the four principles under study in the Sixth Committee, and also the statements delivered during the debates by the representatives of member states. I suggest that a perusal of these comments and statements attests both to the competence of the jurists involved in the debate and to the interest of the governments they represent in ensuring the orderly development of principles of international law. More significantly, however, the comments and statements reveal both wide areas of agreement upon what might be termed traditional concepts of international law, and also sharp divergencies on principles that many of us in Western countries are inclined to take as settled law. In the light of the tremendous importance of the U.N. Charter, as perhaps the greatest law-making treaty in the history of man, it is essential that we be aware of these differences, particularly those concerning the nature and importance of the principles of international law laid down in the U.N. Charter. I am not one of those who suggests that the language of the Charter is so sacrosanct that it is biblical in its timelessness. I do believe, however, most strongly, that any changes in the interpretation to be placed upon the principles enshrined in the Charter should only be brought about knowingly and after careful deliberation by the member states bound by the treaty known as the Charter. It is precisely on this issue that we must, I fear, continue to take issue with the proponents of the "principles of co-existence" as the "new international law." The need for the continuing development and elaboration of areas of international law is self-evident to any student of the subject. Law is only law when it is enforceable, and it is only enforceable when it genuinely reflects the will of the community, in this case the community of nations. We must, therefore, continue to be responsive to the demands of some of the newer nations of the world to have a part in the shaping and development of the world order in which they live. By the same token, however, if we are genuinely concerned with the continuing evolution of a world order, we must, while attempting to take a positive and dynamic approach to those areas of the law in need of development, continue to be cautious towards any inroads upon those fundamental principles of international law, chief amongst which I would list as the obligation of member states to settle their disputes by peaceful means. It is with respect to this principle, I would suggest, particularly its implementation through increased development and usage of international tribunals such as the International Court of Justice and the International Court of Arbitration, wherein we might usefully concentrate our efforts. It is precisely here, of course, where the greatest differences exist between Western and Soviet bloc jurists. I am hopeful, however, that the fact-finding study agreed on by the U.N. may be a step in bridging these differences. Agreement on this measure is only a first step, of course, but there will be others, and Canada will continue to play an active role in promoting such developments.

I should like, in conclusion, to make known a recent development of interest to Canadians concerned with these important legal issues. Canada has been named by the President of the General Assembly of the U.N. to the twenty-seven-member Special Committee on Principles of International Law concerning Friendly Relations and Co-operation among States, the establishment of which was agreed to at the Eighteenth Session of the U.N. in the fall of 1963*. This Special Committee is charged with the task of drawing up a "report containing, for the purpose of the progressive development and codification of the four principles," previously referred to, and "so as to secure their more effective application," conclusions and recommendations which would take into account (*a*) the practice of the U.N. and of states in the application of the principles

*Resolution No. 1966 (XVIII) of December 30, 1963.

established in the Charter of the United Nations; (*b*) the comments of governments on this subject; and (*c*) the views and suggestions of member states during the Seventeenth and Eighteenth Sessions of the General Assembly. Membership on this Committee provides Canada with an opportunity to continue to develop the approach which I have described, with a view to playing a constructive part in the U.N. studies of these fundamental principles of international law.

The Changing Soviet Union: Implications for Canadian Foreign Policy

BLAIR SEABORN

IT SHOULD BE APPARENT to every intelligent observer of international affairs that an important segment of the foreign policy problems of the Western nations, and therefore of Canada, derives directly or indirectly from our relations with the communist world and the activities of the communist powers. The problem of Germany and Berlin is that of the interrelationship of the North Atlantic partnership and the Soviet bloc at the point where they overlap, and of the permanence or otherwise of the spheres of influence and control which emerged as a result of World War II. The multitudinous problems of armaments and disarmament derive directly from the lack of confidence on the part of the two super-powers and their allies as to the other's intentions. The problem of the relationship between the industrially advanced, prosperous, white nations of Europe and America and the economically underdeveloped, poor, black or brown or yellow nations of Asia and Africa is *sui generis*, but it is made more complex by the fact of competition for influence in these latter countries by both the communist and non-communist powers. Even, for Canada, the problem of its relationship with the United States of America is influenced and complicated by the communist fact, as witness North American air defence, trade with the communist countries and the recognition of Communist China. Given this pervasive importance of the communist powers, it is clearly central to the formation of any Western country's foreign policy that it be based on as wise an appreciation as possible of the nature of the communist world, the policy the communists would like to pursue towards the West, and their ability, in military, economic, and political terms, to pursue such a policy. Hence the tremendous amount of research and analysis, both governmental and private, devoted in the West to communist affairs.

I hope that the title of my essay, "The Changing Soviet Union: Implications for Canadian Foreign Policy," will not be considered a misleading one if I say that I do not intend to enunciate *a* policy, let alone *the* policy, which Canada should pursue towards the Soviet Union and its allies. The enunciation of such a policy is clearly the responsibility of the government, not that of a civil servant. What I would like to do, however, is to suggest briefly certain of the changes in the domestic and foreign policy of the U.S.S.R. which have relevance for our own foreign policy. In doing so, I hope to indicate not only the opportunities these changes offer but also the limitations they impose.

There is among students of the Soviet scene one school of thought which says that nothing of real significance *to the West* has changed in the Soviet Union in the last ten years. That school maintains that, as long as the Soviet leaders adhere to their belief in the ultimate victory of communism, as long as they express a willingness to aid and abet this "inevitable" movement of history, as long as they refuse free elections in the countries of Eastern Europe within their sphere of influence, and as long as they dispose of an arsenal sufficient to blow a good part of the Western world to Kingdom come—then so long is it impossible to come to any sort of agreement on important issues, let alone a *modus vivendi* with the U.S.S.R. At the other extreme, there is the school of thought which says that there has taken place in the last ten years such a fundamental change in the thinking of the Soviet leaders that their statements concerning belief in communism and its ultimate triumph throughout the world are now mere lip-service; that their great military strength could not conceivably under any circumstances be used in either a military or a political way against us; and that, throwing off old shibboleths, all that is needed is a generous gesture of comprehension on our part and an offer of concessions, in order to have the Soviet Union settle down in national and ideological harmony, in unequivocal "live-and-let-live," with the rest of the world. Few Western policy-makers would, in fact, be likely to base their actions exclusively on either of these two extreme analyses, total reliance on which, should they be mistaken, could be dangerous for Western policy. They are more likely to choose a more middle-of-the-road interpretation, tending now towards one limit, now towards the other as circumstances change and opportunities offer or disappear.

Keeping in mind these two extremes of interpretation as the outside limits of our enquiry, what changes of significance to the West have taken place in Soviet domestic and foreign policy in the last ten years, that is, for want of a better landmark, since the death of Stalin and the beginning of the rise of Khrushchev to his position of ascendancy in the Soviet leadership? Let us look at just a few of them.

Domestic changes first, and within that field, the economy. Here the most important change has been not just the high rate of increase in industrial output but the growing complexity of the Soviet economy. The change has been from an economy measuring its successes by the relatively unsophisticated toting up of energy units and tons of steel produced, to an economy with a growing variety of goods produced, a growing concern with quality as opposed to sheer quantity and a nascent but very lively concern over real costs and a rational pricing system. The growing complexity of the economy has led to an almost continuous changing of the industrial-bureaucratic structure, the link between Moscow's authority and the factory manager, in an attempt to maintain the principle of centralized planning (and, of course, to avoid the use of price as the regulator of business and industrial activity), while encouraging the initiative and scope for local factory managers and local planning officials which is needed to produce both quality and quantity with efficiency. In the attempt to find the new way, planners and doers have been enabled and indeed encouraged to study even Western capitalist models, and at least one serious Soviet study has been made of the possible adaptation of a modified profit system to a state-controlled economy. The resultant exposure of a growing number of managerial class to Westerners and to Western ideas and techniques is bound, at the very least, to give them a better idea of the economic realities of the West and thereby to make more difficult the job of the Soviet propagandist who would distort the picture for his own purposes.

We hear a great deal these days about the comparative growth rates of the Soviet economy and the economies of the leading Western nations. A lot also is written about Soviet resource allocation problems—the old problem of choice between competing ends for an impatient Mr. Khrushchev who wants to press ahead on all fronts at once. How can he, in fact, at one and the same time, maintain a high rate of defence expenditure and an expensive space programme, maintain or even increase economic and military aid to the under-developed countries, continue a high rate of investment in traditional industries, vastly increase investments in the chemical industry, and improve the lot of the consumer by producing more consumer durables and better housing? Particularly, how can he do this when, according to figures recently released by the United States Central Intelligence Agency, his reserves of gold are low and when, as last year's disastrous harvest only served to point up in a drastic way, agriculture remains the Achilles heel of the Soviet enonomy, the weak point which holds back progress in other fields, requires vast new investment and, this autumn, led to large expenditures of scarce foreign exchange to prevent the diet of the Soviet citizens from becoming even more restricted? The answers to these difficult questions are not yet available, but the decisions which are made about resource allocation in the Soviet Union are clearly important for us in the West. And to the extent that Mr. Khrushchev is willing and able to rely on the West as a supply source, if only to a limited degree, there are important implications for Western policy-makers who must decide what goods they are willing to sell to the U.S.S.R., what form of credits, if any, they are willing to extend, and what Soviet exports they are willing and able to take in repayment.

Secondly, in the domestic field, there is the change which is probably most important for the mass of the Soviet people, those of both high and low estate—the end of the terror, the virtual disappearance of the camps, and the severe limitation on the powers of the secret police. It may be argued that this change derived from no more than a recognition on Khrushchev's part that such methods were no longer (if they ever had been) efficacious, that free labour worked better than slave, that people reacted better to the carrot of material incentives than to the stick of fear and arrest and camp and worse. Whatever the reason, the fact is important that internal methods have changed and improved, and the longer the present methods persist the harder it is to turn the clock back. In political terms there is nothing, of course, remotely akin to an organized and loyal opposition to those presently holding the reins of power, certainly no organized opposition to the system itself, and not even an established method to provide for the vitally important matter of succession within the system. Yet, however great the manipulative power of propaganda may be, and however rudimentary "public opinion" may be, we have in the Soviet Union a relationship between governors and governed in which the former are increasingly recognizing the necessity of taking into account the wishes and opinions of the latter and of persuading rather than merely decreeing.

Because of these changes in the internal scene, there is growing up in the Soviet Union an increasingly complex society with a widening knowledge of the outside world and with (at least in an élite group) a growing sophistication of thought and taste. This process has its excitement and fascination for the Western observer as he follows developments in the theatre, the novel, poetry, and even the visual arts of the U.S.S.R. The striving of the intellectuals and creative artists for a greater measure of freedom of thought and expression has had its ups and downs, but there is nevertheless a net progression over the last ten years, and this has its political significance as well. It is wise, however, not to exaggerate. The ignorance, the distortion of notions about the outside world, are still very great, thanks to state-controlled mass information media whose avowed purpose is to mould and guide, not to inform in an objective sense. The number of those who are able to establish contact with foreigners is still small, and controlled, and of those who are able to travel abroad smaller still. The Communist Party is still omnipresent, overseeing and directing, or at least attempting to direct, every aspect of human activity. The Soviet Union is still far from being a pluralistic society—though there are certain of the preconditions which may eventually make for pluralism. Insofar as Western policy is concerned, the modest aim has been to encourage, by means of the exchange of persons and information, a fuller understanding of the Western world by the people and the leaders of the U.S.S.R. Most Western policy-makers would agree that it is in our interest that the Soviet people should be more correctly informed as to our life and aspirations and intentions and that in the broadest sense it is in their true interests as well.

Let us now look briefly at some of the changes which have taken place in the field of Soviet foreign policy over this last ten years.

The change of fundamental importance is the recognition of the virtual impossibility, under present circumstances, of considering the pursuit of policy by means of general, let alone thermonuclear, war. Given the present strategic balance, even a first strike initiative by the U.S.S.R. would leave intact sufficient American retaliatory power to inflict an altogether unacceptable level of damage on the U.S.S.R. The understanding by the Soviet leaders of this basic equation has led to the elaboration of a foreign policy stand to which they have given the name of "peaceful co-existence." Mr. Khrushchev himself has described it as "a form of intense economic, political, and ideological struggle of the proletariat against the aggressive forces of imperialism in the international field," and elsewhere it has been described as "the struggle of the working class . . . for the triumph of socialist [communist] ideas."

Obviously the rejection of major war as an instrument of policy by our chief potential antagonist is of great importance, but in our relief at accepting this as fact, we must keep two other considerations in mind when formulating Western policy. One is that a substantial weakening in the ability or the demonstrable willingness of the West to resist aggression, or a scientific break-through by the Russians which would significantly alter the present balance, *could* alter the Soviet view of the unacceptability of major war or threat of major war. The other is that, having arrived at a strategic situation of mutual deterrence, we still face a keen and often ruthless competition with the communist powers in the fields of politics, economics, and ideology. We cannot relax, but we must be prepared to meet the challenge in these new fields as we have met it in the military sphere.

Another change which is important is the apparently final rejection of the isolationism of the Soviet Union during a large part of Stalin's reign. This is more than just the inevitable increase in influence in world affairs of a country which is now the second largest power on earth. It is a deliberate decision to play a part, to have its word to say on virtually every world problem. The United States of America's interests are world-wide, and so are those of the U.S.S.R., on national as well as ideological grounds. Thus Western policy-makers must learn to accept and cope with the fact that the Soviet Union will be almost obliged to have a thumb in every pie. It will not react more reasonably if the West questions its right to put its thumb in, though this does not mean that the West should meekly let the Soviet Union pull plums out at will.

There is also, in the emergence from isolation, a demand for the respect and the status which the Soviet leaders feel should be accorded them and their country. Their truculence at times may spring from a feeling that they are being slighted or taken too much for granted. It is important that we do not unintentionally give them this cause for complaint, and that we take into account the understandable touchiness of a country which was for so long treated as an outcast and a pariah. But the corollary of this is that we have an obligation to point out what are the modes of civilized behaviour which must govern those who would be accepted fully into the comity of nations.

A third change which is important in the foreign, or at least the external field, to use the Canadian nuance, is the changing nature of the relationships within the communist world: the emergence of the Sino-Soviet dispute, its effects on the bloc and the non-bloc communist parties, and the evolution of the relations between Moscow and the capitals of the Eastern European communist countries. The communist world is no longer, if indeed it ever was, monolithic, or controlled in every aspect of its activity by the omniscient mind in Moscow. We face a number of communist countries, which have their communism and other common interests and obligations to bind them together for main purposes, but which also display varieties of communist experience and a sense of national peculiarity and independence greater than might have been thought possible even a very few years ago. At very least, the implication of this growing diversity is that it is no longer adequate to have *a* policy towards the communist world; it is necessary to tailor and vary one's policy to the various parts of that world and to recognize that relations may be better with one part of it than with another.

Myths and preconceptions die hard, and images of foreign countries often tend to lag behind the realities. It is unwise, even dangerous, to base one's policy on preconceptions and old images unrevised to take change into account. I have tried to suggest, very briefly and in general terms, some of those changing aspects of the Soviet Union which seem to me to be relevant for the Western policy-maker. He will be missing out on opportunities if he fails to realize that change is taking place; and he may be in serious trouble if he overestimates the extent to which change has occurred. There was, after all, a Berlin crisis in the summer of 1961 and a Cuba crisis in the autumn of 1962, and it would be a rash man, certainly a rash policy-maker, who based all his plans on the assumption that similar crises cannot and will not occur again. The challenge from the Soviet Union is a changing one, and even if crises of this nature are not to occur again, it is well to remember that it is still a challenge.

Canadian Initiatives in East-West Legal Relations in the United Nations

J. ALAN BEESLEY

DEVELOPMENTS AFFECTING East-West relations in legal
and quasi-legal fields in recent years have been so rapid and
so diverse that it is hardly possible to comment on all those
questions of interest, such as the attempts to develop legal
rules applicable to outer space, the dispute concerning
financial responsibility of U.N. members for U.N. peace-
keeping measures, the legal aspects of disarmament, and
the current studies of the International Law Commission.
The comments which follow therefore relate chiefly to the
continuing debate concerning the feasibility and utility of
attempting to codify the so-called "principles of co-existence." In selecting this question for discussion it is not
suggested that it is necessarily of pre-eminent importance,
but rather that its examination provides a useful and
perhaps even essential background against which a number
of less diffuse and more concrete topics can be considered.

There seems to be little doubt that Soviet legal theory
is now well into a new phase. Vyshinsky and all his works

have been rejected. A vigorous campaign for the codification of the "principles of co-existence" has been launched. In attempting to determine what is involved in this new approach, it is useful to refer to an official Soviet definition of international law as laid down in a recent textbook on international law published by the Soviet Academy of Sciences, which reads as follows: "International law can be defined as the aggregate of rules governing relations between states in the process of their conflict and co-operation, designed to safeguard their peaceful co-existence, expressing the will of the ruling classes of these states, and defended in the case of need by coercion applied by states individually or collectively." Western jurists may, perhaps be forgiven if at first sight they are struck more by the similarities than the dissimilarities between the Vyshinsky definition and the current one.

The notion of class warfare is also still clearly evident, as is the view of law as an instrument of policy; the reference to coercion by states is somewhat difficult to reconcile with the clear-cut repudiation in a recent issue of *Pravda* of Vyshinsky's emphasis on coercion as a primary element in law; the major innovation, of course, is the emphasis on the concept of peaceful co-existence which is apparently central to the current U.S.S.R. view of international law.

It should not be thought that these issues are purely theoretical abstractions devolving sometimes into mere questions of semantics; Soviet legal theory has always been of significance to Western nations; this is especially true in the light of the strong efforts by the Soviet bloc (which will be referred to later) to persuade other states, indeed all the member-states of the U.N., to accept such theories, in particular the concept of peaceful co-existence. It is, as a consequence, necessary to consider what the term "peaceful co-existence" represents to the U.S.S.R.

The concept has strong ideological overtones, as appears

from a statement issued in Moscow in December, 1960, by eighty-one communist parties to the effect that "peaceful co-existence of states with differing social systems does not mean a reconciliation between the socialist and bourgeois ideologies. On the contrary, it implies an intensification of the struggle of the working class of all communist parties for the triumph of socialist ideas." This highly political interpretation received the imprimatur of Mr. Khrushchev in a statement issued not long afterwards in which he proclaimed that "the policy of peaceful co-existence is a form of intense economic, political, and ideological struggle of the proletariat against the aggressive forces of imperialism in the international field." Such pronouncements suggest that whatever peaceful co-existence may represent as a political concept to various non-communist states, particularly some of the less-developed countries who appear to have espoused the doctrine, it is wise for us to bear in mind that, as pointed out by the Secretary of State for External Affairs, the Hon. Paul Martin, in an address given to the Montreal Section of the Canadian Branch of the International Law Association on October 2, 1963, "From our point of view, the Soviet doctrine of peaceful co-existence may be said to comprise two main elements: (*a*) it provides a doctrinal basis for Soviet bloc assistance to the world revolutionary movement and for the extension of Soviet influence; and (*b*) it provides a doctrinal basis for the Soviet bloc in its relations with non-communist countries, both Western and non-aligned, while the revolutionary process is going on." Mr. Martin went on to suggest that "It is clearly in the interest of non-communist countries to encourage the second of these two elements and to discourage as much as possible the first. . . . For the time being, however, no non-communist country can afford to overlook the first element of the doctrine of peaceful co-existence."

In attempting to translate such a highly political concept

into understandable legal terms, it is useful to refer to the explanations given by the leading exponent of the Soviet version of co-existence, Professor Gregory Tunkin, Legal Adviser to the Foreign Ministry of the U.S.S.R. In his lectures at The Hague in 1958, which may still be taken as an exposition of the official Soviet view, Professor Tunkin stressed the following points: firstly, the embracement of the five so-called principles of peaceful co-existence, namely, sovereignty, non-aggression, non-intervention, equality of states, and peaceful co-existence, itself. Of these, only the principle of sovereignty and the concept of peaceful co-existence would seem to be distinctive of Soviet legal theory; the first because it exemplifies the classical or nineteenth-century "quasi-absolute" concept of sovereignty stressed by the Soviet Union from the time of its earliest writers, as distinguished from the more generally accepted notion of sovereignty subjecting it to the rule of law amongst nations (for example, as will be illustrated later, Soviet legal theory rejects such institutions as third party arbitration or compulsory acceptance of jurisdiction of the International Court of Justice as infringements of sovereignty); the concept of peaceful co-existence is, in Soviet legal theory, according to a statement published in *Izvestia* in April, 1962, by three eminent Russian professors of international law, a "Leninist concept comprising a specific form of the class struggle between capitalism and socialism." This affirmation of the bi-polarization of the world on the basis of two "diametrically opposed" economic systems, seemingly represents an attempt to rationalize international law with Marxism, and not the converse.

Other notable characteristics of Soviet legal theory as expounded by Professor Tunkin may be summarized as including: the elevation of treaties over custom as the primary source of international law; a treaty-like approach to customary international law, whereby a norm's validity is confined to those states explicitly recognizing it as binding; the explanation of international law as a system of norms created by a collision of wills of ruling classes of different states, rather than as a set of normative principles to which states are subject; the rejection of "supra-nationalism" as an unacceptable limitation of state sovereignty and, hence, utopian; the relegation of the decisions of the International Court of Justice to a very subsidiary position as a source of international law; and the appropriation of widely recognized principles of international law as Soviet inspired and developed.

It can readily be seen that there are a number of important differences between Western and Soviet approaches to international law. In commenting on the latter, Mr. Paul Martin in his speech previously referred to, suggested that "It may be wondered whether such theories are not fundamentally inimical to the future development of international law along orderly lines."

What has made these theories of particular importance to us is the efforts carried out by the Soviet bloc in a number of governmental and non-governmental forums to bring about the codification of the "principles of co-existence."

As early as 1954, during the general conference of U.N.E.S.C.O., Soviet bloc representatives urged joint legal research between East and West on peaceful co-existence. Later the topic was raised in 1957 and again in 1958 in the General Assembly of the U.N., and in each case rejected as a specific topic for study. On the first occasion the U.S.S.R. introduced into the First Committee of the U.N. the item "Declaration concerning the Peaceful Co-existence of States." An alternative resolution introduced by India, Sweden, and Yugoslavia entitled "Peaceful and Neighbourly Relations among States" was passed in its stead. On the second occasion, Czechoslovakia requested that an item entitled "Measures aimed at the Implementation and Promotion of Principles of Co-existence among States" be placed on the agenda of the General Assembly; the item adopted instead substituted the phrase "Peaceful and Neighbourly Relations" for that of "Peaceful Co-existence."

At the Sixteenth Session of the U.N. the topic "Juridical Aspects of Peaceful Co-existence" was proposed by Czechoslovakia and a number of other countries for inclusion in the agenda of the Sixth Committee. After considerable debate a resolution was passed substituting the phrase "Friendly Relations and Co-operation among States" for "Peaceful Co-existence."

During the Seventeenth Session of the U.N. a draft resolution containing a "Declaration of Principles of International Law" was tabled by the Czechoslovakian Delegation listing nineteen principles, including the well-known "principles of co-existence." A resolution emphasizing the importance of the rule of law amongst nations (rather than peaceful co-existence) and advocating the study of specific areas of the law in need of development and elaboration rather than the codification of general principles was tabled by Canada and a number of other delegations. The resolution ultimately adopted, after considerable general debate and subsequently lengthy negotiations between the delegations of Canada, Czechoslovakia, and Yugoslavia (which had also filed a resolution on the question) decided on a legal study of four principles, namely the duty to refrain from the threat or use of force, the principle of peaceful settlement of disputes, of non-intervention in domestic jurisdiction, and of sovereign equality of states. The resolution also affirmed the importance of the Charter of the U.N. in the continuing development of the rule of law among nations, but contained no reference to peaceful co-existence.

In the Eighteenth Session of the U.N., in the autumn of 1963, the debate continued on the four topics referred to, with the Soviet bloc delegation once again stressing the "principles of co-existence" as the basis of the "new international law." The resolution eventually adopted agreed to the establishment of a sub-committee of the U.N. for the further study of these principles, once again with no reference to the concept of co-existence.

In the meantime, the subject had been introduced into the discussions of the International Law Association at the 1956 Conference at Dubrovnik, in a paper presented by Professor Bartos of Yugoslavia. The question was subsequently discussed by the Co-existence Committee, during the 1958, the 1960, and the 1962 Conferences of the I.L.A., thus far with no definitive conclusions. The debate continues, in the I.L.A. as in the U.N.

The foregoing brief outline of Soviet bloc efforts to have the "principles of co-existence" codified indicates the importance the communist countries attach to this matter.

It may, before concluding, be useful to consider how these principles are applied to certain topical questions. One example of continuing interest and importance is the efforts being made to bring about world disarmament. Such a complex subject can hardly be discussed adequately in the time and space available, but one or two illustrations may be helpful.

In an article by O. V. Bogdanov, which appeared in the September, 1963, issue of the journal *Soviet State and Law*, it is stated that "a solution of the problem of security of states in a disarmed world should be sought in the universally recognized principles of modern international law with the use of mechanisms to prevent violations of peace as envisaged in the United Nations Charter." This statement would appear to be consistent with the joint statement of the U.S.S.R. and the U.S.A. of agreed principles for disarmament negotiations of September 20, 1961, which reads in part "that such disarmament is accompanied by the establishment of reliable procedures for the peaceful settlement of disputes and effective arrangements for the maintenance of peace in accordance with the principles of the Charter of the U.N." Later it is provided in the agreed principles "that states shall support and provide agreed manpower for U.N. peace forces"; later again it is stated that "to implement control over and inspection of disarmament, an international disarmament organization, including all parties to the agreement, should be created within the framework of the U.N." Another passage from the agreed principles provides that "progress in disarmament should be accompanied by measures to strengthen institutions for maintaining peace and the settlement of international disputes by peaceful means," and the necessary measures to do so are stated as "including the obligation of states to place at the disposal of the U.N. agreed manpower necessary for an international peace force to be equipped with agreed types of armaments."

The article by Bogdanov previously referred to goes on, after his opening statement, to say that "the Soviet programme of general and complete disarmament . . . rightly turns down the groundless argument that even under complete disarmament international security must be upheld by means of an armed centralized apparatus." The writer criticizes the Western approach to disarmament as being an attempt "to prove the need, in the existing conditions, to replace the now operating international law by a kind of 'world' law, and the U.N. organization by a kind of 'world authority' with extensive rights to employ compulsory measures against states." In Bogdanov's view, "the abolition of arms would decisively affect the very nature of the relations between states, eliminate the material premises which bring about war and hence also the necessity of applying armed force in international relations. This excludes the needs of setting up an unwieldy mechanism of armed constraint and the adoption as a basic thesis of the premise that the security of states in a disarmed world can be guaranteed by the generally recognized principles of international law." In case it is felt that this represents a radical shift in the Soviet approach to the International Court of Justice, the writer states in a later passage that "the desire to use the International Court of Justice as a medium for the establishment of a 'world' law is typical of present day imperialist practices and for many Western lawyers who reflect this practice. The imperialist powers are banking on their majority in the International Court of Justice, reckoning that in the face of its becoming a body of binding jurisdiction they would be able to channel the development of international law in accordance with their wishes." Such Western jurists as Larsen, Clark, Sohn, and Fisher are all criticized in the article on the ground that they "want a 'world government' endowed with extensive legal and executive powers upon the people" which will "be established to dominate undividedly in a disarmed world," and that "they want relations between disarmed states to hinge on 'supra-national' enforcement which they consider to be an indispensable element in the operation of 'world' law." Bogdanov concludes that "any attempt to find some kind of contradiction between the conditions which still prevail in a disarmed world and the nature of the vital principles of present-day international law, such as sovereignty, equality of states, non-interference in their domestic affairs, and so forth, is profoundly artificial in their character. Disarmament will in no way undermine these principles; on the contrary, it will create the most favourable conditions for their consistent realization." The relationship between Soviet legal theory and the Soviet approach to this concrete issue is clearly evident.

Turning to another area of the law, a good deal of attention has been focussed recently upon the proposal by Mr. Khrushchev for an international agreement on the non-use of force to determine border controversies. An interesting exposition of the legal basis of this proposal was given in an article by Professor Tunkin, published in *Izvestia* on August 22, 1963, which reads in part: "Marxism-Leninism has proceeded from the proposition that border issues must be solved on the basis of the self-determination of nations." Lenin is quoted as stating that "an annexation is a violation of the self-determination of a nation, is the establishment of the border of a state contrary to the wish of the population." Professor Tunkin goes on to relate these principles to current issues: "In relations between the countries of the world socialist system, resting on the principle of socialist internationalism, there are possibilities of settling a border question to the mutual satisfaction of the parties on the basis of friendship and understanding." He goes on to explain, however, that "Imperialism has left behind a great heritage in Asia and especially in Africa," since "the seizure of the colonies and their division among the imperialist states was done by force of arms so that the national borders were naturally not taken into consideration." Nonetheless, he concludes that "any border dispute should be settled only by peaceful means—such is the solely possible answer today dictated by the moral and juridical standards corresponding to the political expediency, expressing the wills of the people and serving the interest of the historical progress." He warns that should the new African nations try and settle their disputes by force of arms, "such a situation would suit only imperialists, it would lead not only to the weakening of the African states' struggle against imperialism, but would create conditions for these states' subjection to the imperialist powers for their alignment with the aggressive blocs of the Western powers. The Chinese-Indian armed border conflict is most instructive in this respect. This conflict not only spoiled the relations between India and China, not only hampered the struggle of the progressive forces and stirred the most reactionary forces of India to activity, it created a new hotbed of international tension and hampered the struggle of the Asian peoples against imperialism." Since the announcement of Mr. Khrushchev's proposal, Professor Tunkin has found it necessary to add, in the January 7, 1964, issue of *Izvestia*, that "the principle of banning the use of force in international relations and the principle of a peaceful solution of disputes between states in no away affects the struggle of the peoples of colonial and dependent countries for their liberation. If in this struggle the peoples of the colonial countries are compelled to take up arms against foreign invaders, this is their sacred right. This is the exercise of the right to self-defence recorded in the U.N. Charter."

Such statements by the Legal Adviser to the Foreign Ministry of the U.S.S.R. are of assistance in interpreting developments such as the recent proposals by Mr. Khrushchev. They also provide evidence of the need for caution, referred to by Prime Minister Lester B. Pearson in his recent statement, in assessing the implications of the present improvement in relations.

How then are we to react to these consistent, determined, and often dynamic Soviet initiatives? Firstly, by recalling that international relations are not conducted in a legal vacuum; that over some three centuries a body of customary and conventional principles and rules of law has been developed, against which such proposals should be viewed. See, for example, the selected background documentation prepared by the U.N. Secretariat, to assist in the studies by the Sixth Committee of the four principles previously referred to.*

The first test, therefore, is whether such proposals show promise of making a genuine contribution to the development of international law along orderly lines. It is the view

*U.N. Doc. A/C. 6/L537, dated October 30, 1963.

of most Western nations, for instance, that attempts to codify general principles of international law on a high level of abstraction are of limited usefulness unless coupled with the will and the machinery for applying such principles to concrete tension situations. The fate of the 1949 Draft Declaration of Rights and Duties of States bears witness to the validity of this conclusion. Western and non-aligned nations have, as a consequence, put forth in the Sixth Committee of the U.N., counter-proposals for the further development of specific areas of the law considered central to the future development of international law along orderly lines, and for the further development of the machinery necessary for the peaceful settlement of disputes. It is felt that, quite apart from East-West differences, such studies can assist in determining how best to meet the legitimate desires of many of the non-aligned countries to play a more direct role in the development of international law.

A second test which might be applied is whether the proposals have been raised in the most appropriate forum. If the problem is a highly political one, which only member-states of the U.N. are competent to consider, then the motives in raising it in a private non-governmental organization may be open to question. If, on the other hand, the matter is a technical one, of an essentially legal nature, then it may be through the International Law Commission (of which Mr. Cadieux, the Legal Adviser to the Canadian Ministry of External Affairs, is a member) that qualified experts can best contribute to the progressive development and codification of international law. Other questions falling into neither category might appropriately be considered by the Sixth Committee of the U.N. This is not to suggest, of course, that such studies as are being carried out by the International Law Association, and by other non-governmental groups, concerned with the scientific analysis and development of international law, cannot also make significant contributions to a better understanding of the differences which divide us, and even of possible means of reconciling them. On the contrary, such free and informal discussions of the legal theory of Western and communist nations may not only be of educational value but can play an important role in the law-making process itself.

Let us therefore recognize the desirability of continuing the dialogue; but let us also remind our protagonists that a dialogue by definition should flow two ways; that a demand for the codification of the principles of co-existence, for instance, prejudges the validity of the conception; let us ask for a broader approach; let us ask that such proposals as the U.N. fact-finding study put forth by the Netherlands and co-sponsored by Canada and a number of other countries be received with less suspicion and hostility; let us continue to stress the diversity and complexity of the factors at play in international affairs, and to resist the narrower unilaterally held notion of divergency and of bi-polarization. It is thus that we can play a constructive role in the continuing evolution of world legal order.

It seems clear that there are winds of change blowing through the sometimes dusty halls of international law; equally clearly, they do not emanate from any single source. Consider, for example, the broad spectrum of views, many with possible significance for the future development of international law, presented by governments of member-states of the U.N. in their written comments and in the oral interventions of their representatives during the recently concluded debate of the Sixth Committee of the U.N. Compare, for instance, as further evidence of the diversity of forces at play, the lectures of Professor Tunkin at The Hague with the Encyclical *Pacem in Terris* issued by the late Pope John. (Not surprisingly, the differences may be more readily apparent than the similarities. Pope John wrote on non-intervention, on the requirement of fostering friendly relations in all fields, on the juridical equality of states, self-determination, mutual co-operation, the solution of disputes by negotiation, and other questions dear to the heart of Professor Tunkin. Also, however, he wrote of the principles of natural justice, of the dignity of the individual, and of human rights in terms irreconcilable with Marxism, and called for the development of "a public authority having world-wide power and endowed with the proper means for the efficacious pursuit of its objectives.")

It should be obvious, on the basis of this brief examination of various trends in legal fields, that it is impossible for foreign ministries of Western countries to ignore certain fundamental differences in legal approach, and unwise to minimize them. It seems equally clear, however, as pointed out by Mr. Paul Martin in his speech referred to earlier, that "in the spirit of *détente* following the signing of the Test Ban Treaty there is nothing to be served by attempting to exaggerate these differences of approach to international law. On the contrary, the need is for renewed efforts to bridge the differences."

Canadian Attitudes to Change and Conflict in the Soviet Bloc

H. GORDON SKILLING

PRESIDENT KENNEDY, in a major address at the American University on June 10, 1963, called upon his fellow-Americans to "re-examine our attitude to the Soviet Union" and "our attitude towards the cold war." Six months later, shortly after his tragic death, his Assistant Secretary of State for Far Eastern Affairs, Roger Hilsman, declared that it was time "to take stock . . . dispassionately" of the problem of China, and necessary to discard emotion and "look squarely at China." "Dislike of communism," he said, must "not becloud our ability to see the facts." The Canadian Minister of External Affairs, Paul Martin, has also spoken of "the winds of change blowing over the communist world" and the need to "face the facts of life." In a speech at the Canadian National Exhibition in Toronto, on August 24, 1963, he urged us to "try to understand these changes, for without that understanding we shall be unable to assess the nature of our opponent and of the contest."

It is in the spirit of these remarks that Canada, and the

West generally, should re-examine its attitudes towards the Soviet Union and China, and towards the whole Soviet bloc. The main responsibility for wrestling with these thorny problems must naturally rest with the United States, and Canada does not have the power to affect the outcome decisively. Nonetheless Canada and Canadians are deeply involved, and seriously affected, by the crucial decisions ahead, which should take account of our interests and views and should be such as to be acceptable to us. Moreover, the solution of these complicated questions depends, not merely on the exercise of power, but on understanding and a wise choice of alternatives, and not least on imagination, a commodity which is not a monopoly of any Western nation. Indeed, that most perceptive American, George Kennan, in his article on the theme, "Polycentrism and Western Policy"* has warned publicly of the danger of "lack of imagination" in the West in dealing with the problem of communist diversity.

What is the reality of the present-day communist world, to which the Western countries are required to make response? This has been often expounded by the academic and other experts, not least ably by George Kennan in the article just cited. There he describes "the recent disintegration of that extreme concentration of power in Moscow which characterized the communist bloc," and the "emergence in its place of a plurality of independent or partially independent centres of political authority within the bloc" —in a word, of "polycentrism." In the ten years since the death of Stalin, and particularly in the years since the Hungarian revolt and the Polish resistance in 1956, the once unified Soviet bloc has been undergoing momentous change, the tempo of which has been accelerated by the Sino-Soviet conflict of the past five years. No longer do we face a monolithic bloc, dominated by Moscow and hewing

*42 *Foreign Affairs* 171 (1964).

to a common course in world affairs. Indeed in a very real sense there is no longer a single Soviet bloc, or a single international communist movement, but instead, two blocs and two movements, headed by Moscow and Peking and locked in deadly rivalry and conflict. The tenuous bonds that still link the two competing associations cannot conceal, or contain, the mutual antagonisms. Even if the "rift" does not become an open split, it can never be sufficiently bridged to restore the original unity and uniformity of Stalin's day. In the house of communism there are and will remain many mansions; the Stalinist skyscraper is a thing of the past.

In some respects the situation of the communist world is better described, not as polycentrism, but as bi-centrism, or to use another term, bi-polarism. In terms of power and the capacity of fully independent policy, there are really only two "poles of power," namely Moscow and Peking. Around them have grouped their subordinate allies—around Moscow, all the Eastern European states, except for Albania, but including Yugoslavia, and Outer Mongolia; and around Peking, the remaining Asian states, North Korea and North Vietnam, and Albania. In other words, a kind of balance of power has emerged within the communist bloc. Nevertheless, even the smaller participants in this balance have attained a limited independence, a certain freedom of manoeuvre not unlike that possessed by any small power associate of a great power. Yugoslavia, for instance, although basically accepting Soviet foreign policies, has her own non-aligned version of co-existence. Poland has taken a limited degree of initiative, in particular in its oft-repeated proposals for a nuclear freeze in Central Europe. Roumania has held to a course of its own in Comecon relations, insisting on its right to a full and rounded industrial development, including the promotion of heavy industry. Even little Albania, although now following closely the Chinese course, has shown its ability to reject the main trend of Soviet policies. Moreover, most of these smaller associates of the two great communist powers no doubt possess a greater capacity for independent action than they normally exercise. In critical future decisions, their actions may demonstrate this now partly hidden ability. There is therefore an important element of truth in the polycentrism of the communist world, parallelling the even more pronounced polycentrism of the Western world.

Another aspect of polycentrism is the increasing differentiation of policy within each of the states of communism. "National communism" is an undeniable fact. This has been expressed in differing degrees of de-Stalinization, and more broadly, in an intensifying diversity of domestic patterns. The doctrine of the "many paths to socialism," once a heresy within world communism, has now become accepted doctrine, and indeed increasingly a reality. Not merely Yugoslavia, the original exponent of the doctrine, but other states, such as Poland and Hungary, have been able to follow a much more autonomous course in domestic affairs. China, too, in her own way, has forged a distinctive communist way of life, no longer modelled slavishly on the Soviet pattern. Some states, such as Roumania, East Germany, and until recently, Czechoslovakia, have distinguished themselves from the Soviet Union and from the others, chiefly in their effort to maintain the Stalinist system intact, while paying lip-service to de-Stalinization. Even in Czechoslovakia, however, the long-term impact of de-Stalinization has become evident, as veteran Stalinists have been removed from power, and pressures on the régime have brought about substantial liberalization, especially in cultural life. Novotný, hardbitten Stalinist that he is, in these circumstances seeks to evolve a more flexible domestic policy more in tune with Khrushchev's temper and with the yearning of the Czechs and Slovaks. This is not to say that genuine freedom has emerged, or is even around the corner, but these régimes no longer exhibit the same rigidity of action, and under the combined impact of domestic pressures and Moscow example, freer forces have been set loose in society.

Polycentrism has not produced a condition of stability in the communist world, but on the contrary, a state of intense conflict—conflict between communist states, such as China and Soviet Russia, or Albania and Yugoslavia; conflict within states, among the leaders, between Stalinists and de-Stalinizers, or between proponents of Peking and Moscow, and between people and régimes; and above all, conflict within the U.S.S.R., between Khrushchev and his opponents or lukewarm supporters. It can hardly be assumed that the conflicts will soon cease, or that the polycentrist situation will settle down in a fixed status quo. Indeed there is conflict within the soul of many a communist leader, including Khrushchev himself, and still more, the subordinate leaders of Eastern Europe. There is what Kennan so aptly terms "a great crisis of indecision," especially over the proper attitude to be taken towards Moscow's policies; towards Peking; towards Albania and Yugoslavia; and above all, towards the West, and particularly Washington. In many ways, the central point at issue between Peking and Moscow is the attitude to be adopted towards the United States and its allies in the coming years on a host of fundamental questions of policy. Uncertainly, and hesitantly, certain communist leaders, notably Khrushchev and his supporters, are feeling their way towards some degree of rapprochement with the U.S.A., and others, notably the Chinese, have maintained their traditional hostility towards that power. The death of Kennedy stirred up again uncertainty and soul-searching over this issue, and at the same time clearly demonstrated the profound difference of views within the communist bloc in its estimate of Western policy, and the possibility of living with it. Chinese school children rejoiced over the tragic event, whereas in Poland all flags were flown at half-mast.

One last point in this sketch of the realities of world communism as they present themselves in 1964. The events described have naturally greatly weakened the communist states in the world balance of power, dividing their military and economic strength, weakening their political and ideological appeal, and forcing them to devote their attention to bloc and domestic conflicts. The public polemic between China and Soviet Russia in particular has worried the leaders, especially the Poles, who have been devoting much effort to the promotion of private discussions to settle some of the controversial questions. Mieczyslaw F. Rakowski, editor-in-chief of the leading Polish political weekly, *Polityka*, in his paper on November 23, 1963, referring to the change in the balance of power to the advantage of the communist world in the post-war period, wrote: "A decisive element which made these changes in the balance of power possible was the unity of the socialist countries, the unity of the whole communist movement. The continuing successes in the field of perpetuating world peace and strengthening the position and authority of socialism closely depend on whether the socialist countries continue to oppose imperialism as one body, motivated by one thought and propelled by one aim, guided by a single and co-ordinated foreign policy." In the same way, he went on, the defence of the security of the communist countries was to be attained "only under the conditions of unity of the socialist countries." Clearly implicit in his remarks was the conclusion that, conversely, disunity is damaging the security and the diplomatic effectiveness of the communist countries.

For the West these changes within the communist world have brought solid advantages—a weakening of the general

strength of the once united communist world, the emergence
of a more liberal concept of communism in the Moscow
group, and the beginning of a more conciliatory and flexible
foreign policy, making possible some negotiated agreements
with the West. At the same time, there is the danger
threatening from an isolated and aggressive China, unre-
stricted by the limiting effects of its alliance with the U.S.S.R.,
and perhaps therefore encouraged to embark on dangerous
courses of its own. This has begun to produce in some
quarters in the West a recognition of the desirability of a
response to these events that will not discourage, but rather
give whatever encouragement is possible, to the tendencies
towards independence, liberalization, and conciliation
within the communist bloc, while at the same time seeking
to avoid the total isolation of China and to encourage it to
moderate its policies.* There are even some signs that official Washington is beginning to understand the opportunities presented by the new situation and the necessity of
adopting more flexible and imaginative policies to meet
them, and of holding the door open for evolutionary
changes even in China. Yet American policy is still sub-
jected to severely limiting factors, both in its previous
commitments, and in public attitudes on questions such as
China, and cannot easily adjust its foreign policies to meet
the new situation. There are even those in Congress who
argue that we must take advantage of communist weak-
nesses and disunity to isolate them still further, and in
particular to make no concession to China or even to the
more independent states of Eastern Europe, such as Poland
and Yugoslavia. That there is still much confusion is suggested by a report published in the *New York Times*, on
December 2, 1963, that the Department of State was hopeful that Soviet and Chinese communists might resolve their

---

*See the article by Kennan already cited, and also Donald S. Zagoria,
"The Sino-Soviet Conflict and the West," 41 *Foreign Affairs* 171 (1962).

differences, and was fearful that a rupture might interrupt the trends toward liberalization and independence in Eastern Europe. This report was received with almost incredulity by Professor Alex Dallin, of the Russian Institute, Columbia University, who in a letter to the same paper on December 7, stated the contrary view, namely that the Sino-Soviet conflict was a prerequisite, not an impediment, for effective autonomy and greater diversity in Eastern Europe.

We come at last to the question of Canadian attitudes towards change and conflict in the communist world, especially towards these trends in Eastern Europe. On the whole, Canada has in the past officially adopted a passive, backseat attitude towards these momentous issues, and has publicly offered no independent initiative. On the great questions of world politics, including policies to be adopted towards the communist world and its parts, Canada has been willing to leave matters largely to the United States and Great Britain, France and Germany, offering its own views only in special circumstances and usually in private. This has reflected our recognition of the relatively small influence which Canada can bring to bear on these questions so vitally affecting her own future. It has also reflected Canadian unwillingness to run the risk of alienating the United States on issues regarded by the latter as crucially important and on which popular emotions run high. In the case of Eastern Europe, there have been the additional factors that Canada and Canadians have relatively few and restricted direct interests in these countries, and knowledge of this region is limited. Moreover, a large proportion of our population calls Eastern Europe its homeland, and our postwar emigration has brought strong new reinforcements from this part of the world. Intense feeling among many new Canadians on questions of communism, especially among two of our largest groups, the German and Ukrainian, as well as on traditional national conflicts of Eastern Europe, has been a negative factor inhibiting Canadian policy from an independent initiative and has certainly not encouraged a policy of conciliation towards the Soviet Union or Poland, for instance. A dramatic effort in an opposite direction, the Diefenbaker move in the United Nations in 1962 for promoting the self-determination of the Ukrainians, and citizens of other Eastern European countries, was welcomed by more extreme nationalists among the ethnic groups in Canada, but accomplished little, and only succeeded in alienating the governments of Eastern Europe, including the Soviet Union. A government must certainly tread carefully on issues of this kind, as the U.S.A. has often demonstrated. But foreign policy must not be distorted, or even determined, by sectional or nationality interests and must reflect the national interests of the country as a whole and the common interest of Canada and other countries in the maintenance of peace.

There are some reasons which may be advanced for a Canadian initiative with respect to the communist world, and to Eastern Europe in particular. Our hands are in some ways less tied by previous commitments and political limitations than those of the U.S.A. Our ethnic groups are less capable, under a parliamentary system, of bringing pressure to bear on foreign policy. We are not tied by the same degree of emotionalism among the public on such issues as China and Cuba. We have no China lobby, or John Birch Society, and at the same time, regrettably, a less active and vigorous public discussion of foreign affairs. Moreover, our tradition has been to make diplomacy less a matter of moral idealism and propaganda and more a matter of realism and quiet negotiation. We have also special reasons for understanding the position of the communist states of Eastern Europe. In particular, the way in which they are gradually and carefully feeling their way towards greater independence within the Socialist "Commonwealth" awakens memories of our own not too distant or too different past. Their efforts as smaller powers to escape the enthusiastic embrace of a neighbouring great power, and to remind that power of their existence, of their desire not to be taken for granted, strike a responsive chord in our own experience. Even the dilemma of choosing between two allies, Soviet Russia and China, and their desire to see them moving in unison, reminds us of our own traditional embarrassment in the face of Anglo-American rivalries and conflicts. Reciprocally, the position of Canada is not without understanding and recognition among informed Eastern European leaders—our independent position and our distinctive policies, for instance with reference to China and Cuba, are known and appreciated.

More recently, there have been encouraging signs of a new and refreshing Canadian approach to the communist world and the changes and conflict within it. Most notable, of course, have been the recent wheat deals with China, and later with Soviet Russia, Poland, Czechoslovakia, and Bulgaria. Even more encouraging has been the recognition shown by the Minister of External Affairs, the Hon. Paul Martin, in recent speeches, that the Eastern European states have acquired greater freedom of manoeuvre and are taking national interests more and more into account in their internal policies. In a speech in the House of Commons on November 28, 1963, he expressed the thought that the solution of East-West problems will come "through the slow evolution of communist thinking about their own methods and objectives, and about the outside world. It will not help if the Soviet leaders continue to feel that the West is totally alien and implacably hostile. Breaking down this dangerous misconception is the political reason behind our encouragement of cultural and other contacts, and it should also be the political reason for our trade with communist countries." At the same time, he has, quite rightly, I think, expressed doubt that the isolation of China from the rest of the world is the wisest solution of the problem of dealing with this more recalcitrant member of the bloc. In his speech at the Canadian National Exhibition in Toronto, he stated: "We shall have to ponder very carefully whether an answer to the rising power of Asian communism is to be found in its further isolation and containment, or whether it lies in broadening contacts at a variety of levels in an endeavour to penetrate the curtain of ignorance and blunt the edge of ideological differences." His own mind was, it would seem, already made up on this question, and this was made quite clear in his subsequent Commons speech of November 28, 1963, when he said that "the increasing ostracism of Communist China from the world community may be self-defeating and a potential threat to international stability." "It is not too soon," he went on, "to begin in the West to formulate realistic and far-sighted policies towards this Asian giant." In a more recent utterance, at a press conference in Winnipeg on January 12, 1964, Mr. Martin spoke again of "the dangers of attempting to isolate any communist country, whether it be in Asia, or elsewhere.

What more may Canada do? In general, we should neglect no opportunity, within the limits of our power, to promote the positive force now emerging in the communist bloc, to indicate our own receptive and sympathetic attitude towards it, while at the same time, we should avoid the total isolation and alienation of even the more negative elements in the communist world. The liberalization of the communist régimes and their growing autonomy from Moscow, certainly welcomed by the peoples of those countries, is something we, too, should welcome. Their efforts to work out a new relationship with the West in matters of foreign policy should be greeted with sympathy and understanding, and not crushed by instantaneous rejection and public condemnation, so that the forces making for accommodation and reconciliation are given a supporting hand rather than a slap in the face. At the same time, towards China, we should also hold out the hope of eventual compromise, of recognition of her legitimate interests and international rights. Wherever these matters of high policy are discussed, whether in Moscow or Washington, or in London or Paris, the Canadian voice should be raised in support of a policy of encouraging reason, moderation, and independence in the communist world, and yet of seeking to communicate and to deal with even the more extreme forces, such as the Chinese. Perhaps we may supply an ingredient of "imagination" and "originality," the lack of which has been so obvious in Western policy of the past decade.

More specifically, I think that there are a number of initiatives that might be made, on our own account, and without alienating in any way our friends and allies. In the first place, the "Canadian presence" should be somewhat more emphatically felt in Eastern Europe than at the present time. We have now only four diplomatic missions in that part of the world, and with limited staff. We have embassies in Moscow, Warsaw, Prague, and Belgrade, as well as outside the bloc in Vienna and Athens. There is need for some modest expansion of this representation, not only to make possible widened Canadian knowledge of the area, but also as a symbol of Canada and of Canadian independence in world affairs. This is particularly true of Hungary, where Canadian interests are represented by the British Embassy. My own travels in Eastern Europe gave me the impression that Budapest is one of the most dynamic and interesting of the Eastern European communist capitals. Apart from that, there might be consideration of extending the authority of some of the existing embassies, such as that in Belgrade or a new one in Budapest, to cover neighbouring countries, such as Roumania and Bulgaria. Another useful advance would be the assignment to the Vienna embassy of a political affairs officer, who, like the commercial attaché already there, would have the responsibility of observing Eastern European affairs, and of travelling in the region.

In the second place, a vigorous effort should be made to explore the possibilities of extended commercial exchange with Eastern European countries. Paul Martin has spoken of the possibilities of increasing trade in non-strategic goods with the communist world, including China, and has said that trade has "a special place in the process of overcoming the mistrust which exists between the West and the entire communist bloc." In this respect, Canada has already taken the initiative in the recently concluded wheat agreements, and should press forward towards expanded trade, including, of course, the purchase of commodities to balance communist purchases of our goods. The wheat deals, while serving our own economic interests, have helped to contribute to a clearer image of the independence of Canada in its foreign policy, and have, I am sure, won sympathy for us, not only in the governments, but among the peoples of China, Poland, Czechoslovakia, Bulgaria, and the Soviet Union. What I am urging is the exploring of further possibilities, not only in the countries where we are at present represented, but in others, such as Bulgaria, Roumania, even Albania. This may require some extension of our trade representation, either in Vienna, or—taking a leaf from Germany—in special trade offices in countries where we are not yet represented. This effort should not exclude China, or states supporting her, in Europe or Asia, where, short of diplomatic representation, some form of commercial representation is desirable to facilitate such explorations and negotiations. The commercial boycott of China, as of Cuba, seems to be a blind alley not likely to produce the desired results, and the partial inclusion of

China in the system of world trade a more likely means of wearing down the feeling of isolation.

In the third place, Canada should seek to play a more prominent role in cultural exchanges with the communist bloc. It has not been found possible, nor does it seem necessary, to conclude an inter-governmental cultural agreement with the U.S.S.R. or individual communist countries, along the lines of similar treaties concluded by other Western countries during the past ten years. Nonetheless, there has been a modest amount of cultural exchange, notably the exchange of scientists for short term periods of study and lecturing, between the U.S.S.R. Academy of Sciences and the National Research Board. This year the University of Toronto has exchanged three of its graduate students, all of whom are studying Russian literature in the University of Moscow, for three Soviet scholars (an economist and a physicist, who are conducting research on this campus, and a third, an agronomist, who is studying "meadows" at the Ontario Agricultural College in Guelph). We are now negotiating an exchange of up to five students for next year, and we hope and assume that this will be a permanent academic exchange between the University and the Soviet Ministry of Higher Education. Other universities have also been negotiating with the U.S.S.R. on academic exchanges. There is no reason why this type of academic exchange should not be expanded substantially, either directly or by individual universities, or through an unofficial national committee representing a number of universities. It would be valuable if such exchanges were not confined, as our present exchange agreement is, to doctoral candidates or junior scholars, but were extended to include on the one hand, senior members of the academic staff, and on the other, less advanced graduate students and even undergraduate students, anxious not so much to pursue advanced research as to learn Russian and something of Soviet society.

Even more important would be an extension of the exchange principle to other countries of Eastern Europe, such as Poland or Yugoslavia, following the recent pattern of the United States programme.

Perhaps the time will come, with the precedent of the recently announced cultural agreement with France, when the Canadian government will give some financial support to a broadened programme of cultural exchange with the Soviet Union and other communist countries, providing for the exchange of students, professors, artists, and other persons. Restrictions on travel have recently been relaxed in such countries as Czechoslovakia and Hungary, and travel agencies might well explore the possibilities thus created. Special travel rates for tourists and other visitors from Eastern Europe might facilitate a reciprocal movement in this direction. Indeed, if this exchange is conceived on a people-to-people basis, some thought might be given to an exchange of several hundred individuals or families for a few weeks, on the model of last year's Christmas visit of a Soviet family to an Ohio family. Canadian cities or provinces, or local clubs, might sponsor such visits. Another type of exchange that would be warmly welcomed in Eastern Europe is the exchange of books. During my travel in Eastern Europe I found that every national library desired increased supplies of Canadian books and journals, and would welcome a systematic exchange of materials with our Canadian libraries. These are but examples of the almost unlimited possibilities of communicating with the communist world. In such exchanges, China should not be omitted. Due to the impossibility of travel of U.S. citizens in China, special opportunities present themselves for Canadian scholars or businessmen or artists, provided the Chinese evince a willingness to receive them as guests or tourists, and to exchange persons on a longer run basis for study or travel.

Finally, we must seek steadily to augment our knowledge and information about the communist world, China included, and notably about Eastern Europe. In the past we have been all too dependent in our scholarship and in our mass communications on American and British sources of knowledge on these matters, and this still remains largely the case. This is all the stranger a phenomenon in a country that has increasingly become, not a bi-cultural but a multi-cultural land, with some 25 per cent of its population hailing from Europe, and many of these from those countries of Eastern Europe now under communist rule. We are a country not of two languages, but of many, as a visit to the concert hall or the ski slope will testify. Nonetheless there has been a general neglect of things East European in our schools, in our universities, in our press, radio, and television, and in our cultural life generally. Traditionally our scholarship has been "Western" oriented, concentrating on our British tradition, and with lesser attention to our American neighbours and to Western European languages and civilizations. There has been little study of the Russian language or Russian civilization, let alone of Polish or Yugoslav. Our libraries have been woefully weak in Slavic materials. Research on Eastern Europe or on communism by Canadians is still rare, and even Canadian relations with the Soviet Union and Eastern Europe remain virgin territory for study. Our newspapers, radio, and television have been similarly parochial, with few or no Canadian correspondents in Eastern Europe, even in Moscow. The short-lived Toronto *Globe and Mail* coverage of China by a correspondent in Peking was a refreshing exception. In view of our neglect of the area, our diplomatic representation in Eastern Europe has been surprisingly good, and more than a few of our ambassadors and their colleagues have been able to speak or read Russian, Czech, Polish, or Serbo-Croatian. But the staffs have been small, have often arrived at their posts with little or no linguistic training, have stayed all too short a time (normally two years), and have soon been transferred to other countries or continents, or to other sections of the Department of External Affairs. The situation is changing, at least in the academic realm. During the past fifteen years, programmes of study of Slavic languages and literatures, mainly Russian and Ukrainian, have been developed at the undergraduate and graduate level at universities such as British Columbia, Toronto, and Montreal. More recently, programmes for the broader study of the politics, economics, and history of Russia and Eastern Europe, and of the Soviet world, have been developed, at the undergraduate level at Carleton, and at the graduate level at Alberta. At Toronto, the Centre for Russian and Eastern European studies has recently been established, where staff, funds, library resources and time will hopefully be made available for serious Canadian research on these problems, and where a small corps of specialists may be trained for eventual work as college teachers, diplomats, and journalists. In the Prairie Provinces, the study of Ukrainian has been widely introduced at universities, and as an elective subject even in high schools. The need for the development of international studies, including the intensive study of Russia, Eastern Europe, and China, has been recognized by the Canadian Universities Foundation in its examination, now under way, of academic facilities in this respect. Yet the change has been slow, and even in a relative sense we remain far behind the astonishing blossoming of American programmes for the study of communism and of Russia. Much remains to be done, and the advance should be accelerated. Below the university level, the teaching of the Russian language should be extended in high schools, and, at the universities, special summer programmes for accelerated study of Russian should be available for diplomats, journalists, scholars in the social sciences, high school teachers, and others.

Among many conversations in communist Czechoslovakia,

I had a long one with several of the editors, all Russians, of the journal of world communism, *Problemi mira i sotsialisma*, published in English as the *World Marxist Quarterly*. The editorial offices are located in a former Catholic seminary in Prague, with a large green dome, and over the main doorway, a cardinal's hat, still engraved in stone. This is indeed a holy of holies, a centre of communist orthodoxy, at least from the Soviet point of view, although the paper is no longer published in Chinese or Albanian. Having referred inadvertently to the fact that Canada was a relatively small country, I was at once corrected by the editors who stated firmly that Canada was a great country, and with considerable influence in world affairs. Moreover, they said, they regarded Canada as a distinct nation, with its own distinctive point of view, and following its own policies, as in Cuba and China, different from those of the United States. Although they recognized this fact, they found it difficult to understand in view of the "known" American domination of the economy of the country. My best efforts to try to explain the situation may have been to no avail. The incident nonetheless illustrates the unique and curious role that Canada may play in Eastern Europe. Let us continue to make our presence felt, and to an increasing extent, and let us continue to puzzle and perplex the leaders of communist opinion by our ability to take our own Canadian initiatives towards the individual countries of the communist world.

The Changing Society
of the Soviet Union

MARK GAYN

IN THEIR STUDY of the Soviet Union, our experts all too often use a distorting lens. Some argue that the commissars are the spiritual heirs of the tsars. Others insist that the Soviet Union of Nikita Khrushchev does not differ greatly from the Soviet Union of Josef Stalin. Both, in effect, maintain that the Soviet state and society are evil and unchanging.

If they are right, these historians, sociologists, and political scientists have discovered a new phenomenon— a frozen social system that has successfully defied time and the violence of revolution. Fortunately, there are no such static societies in the modern world. In many respects, the change in the Soviet Union has been even more profound than that in the United States between, say, 1870 and 1910. It has affected every facet of Soviet life—man's relation to man and to authority, social stratification, moods, attitudes, moral values. Far from being frozen, Soviet society is ever-changing, complex, infinitely varied and dynamic.

One need not be in the Soviet Union long to encounter this change, whether in the life of the governed or the behaviour of the governors. All too frequently, the process is violent. But the fact is that Soviet society is still developing its form, codes, and attitudes, and the wrecking of the old still goes on.

Examples of the change abound. In a provincial town not far from Moscow, a mother and her slow-witted son indignantly reject the suggestion that the boy leave school and learn shoemaking. "Never," says the mother in effect. "Never! A technician or a factory worker, yes—but not a cobbler."

The boy is no exception. The residents in his own town must wait for months to have their shoes repaired at the local *ateliers* because the old shoemakers are dying out, and no young men come in to learn the trade. And the town is a microcosm of Soviet society as a whole. Even the dull-witted know this is the age of the technician, the engineer, and the scientist. To these, and not to the shoemaker, go the honour and the reward.

Soviet leaders still glorify manual labour. They extol the strength and stamina of the men and youths who built the great power dams in Siberia; they order school teen-agers to farms and factories for two days each week, ostensibly to teach them respect for manual work. But the new society ignores these moves and sermons. In its new scale of values, manual toil ranks low.

This is merely one example of the changing attitudes that cover the entire spectrum of Soviet life. At its lowest level, this change robs a provincial town of its cobblers; at its highest, it affects political faith and the policies of war and peace.

IT IS ESSENTIAL to understand the causes of this change. In part, it is a by-product of the revolution that destroyed tsarist society. The upheaval eliminated the aristocracy that ruled Russia for centuries, destroyed the immense bureaucracy, wiped out the moneyed men, and played havoc with the middle class. In a way, the new rulers reduced society to one low level, and thus it remained until, inescapably, social chemistry began to work, and stratification began anew.

This process was accelerated by the industrial revolution that was taking place in the land. When Stalin came to power in the late 1920's he faced a society in which three out of every four persons were peasants, and fewer than one in five was a worker or an employee. Stalin then proceeded to flog this mass of ragged and illiterate peasantry into the twentieth century. He bribed or forced the *mujik* to become a townsman; he taught the peasant to use the wrench, the lathe, and eventually the slide-rule; he used monetary incentives, but, even more, he used terror to compel the people to work. And what Stalin seemingly never understood was that it was impossible to convert a backward country into a mighty industrial state without altering the character of society. In the quarter of a century that he remained in power, the number of workers and employees in the nation was doubled. In the same period, the number of engineers and teachers was multiplied roughly fifteen-fold, and the number of economists ten-fold. The country had thus acquired a modern industrial society. Yet Stalin continued to treat his people as if they were still the solid mass of illiterate peasantry he began to govern in the late 1920's. Unwittingly, he had brought into being a complex society that far outgrew his own capacity to comprehend its nature or to govern it wisely.

Years before Stalin died, this society had become dissatisfied and restive. In 1949–50, in one of the worst periods of terror, I lived in Eastern Europe and spoke in confidence to many Soviet and East European intellectuals. Their feelings towards Stalin were compounded of fear, hatred, and contempt. They were frightened and shamed by the barbarism of Stalin's police and political system. They were also depressed by the stark contrast between Stalin's primordial methods of governing and the achievements of the space and nuclear age. Stalin brought the Soviet Union into the twentieth century—the century of advanced technology. But having done that, he and the political machinery he directed became a brake on Soviet development. If nature had not claimed him, an assassin probably would have.

STALIN'S POLITICAL HEIRS understood what he did not. The new society could not be ruled with the old methods. The Soviet Union's twin machinery of governing—the Party and the government—had to be modified; the tight restraints on society had to be eased; the individual had to be given recognition, not in the stilted clichés of *Pravda* editorials (which usually referred to him as The New Soviet Man in The Most Advanced Society in History), but in a measure of freedom to think, speak, and associate.

Thus, Stalin's successors, and especially Nikita Khrushchev, began the immensely complex and politically dangerous process of meeting at least some of the demands of the new society without surrendering the primacy of the Communist Party. Some observers in the West have tended to underestimate the scope of the concessions or the great political subtlety displayed by the rulers. The latter (to paraphrase a familiar phrase) did not fight their way to the communist summit to preside over the dissolution of the Communist Party. But few observers who have lived in the Soviet Union could fail to be startled by the scale (and, at times, the violence) of the change.

In this process, Mr. Khrushchev's famous denunciation of the ghost of Stalin in February, 1956, was an important element. Its purpose, undoubtedly, was to show both the public and the Party cadres that the old methods of government were being abandoned. In making this dramatic demonstration, Mr. Khrushchev and his associates probably realized the risks they were taking—but regarded the risks as justified by the mounting public pressures. The shock treatment led to bloodshed in the streets of Budapest just eight months later. But, though this is not widely appreciated in the West, it also had a shattering impact on Soviet society—an impact that was felt for years.

What is this new Soviet society of the 'sixties? What does it want? What does it fear? What pressures does it exert on its rulers?

It must be understood that the Soviet population is still half urban, half rural; part shockingly backward, part as advanced as any in the world. Despite all the progress that has been made in the countryside, despite the agricultural machinery, the trained managers, agronomists, and accountants, the rural Soviet Union is still half a century behind Saskatchewan or Iowa. Indeed, some prominent Soviet authors have portrayed (and I myself have visited in recent years) villages closer to Tsar Alexander II than to Socialism. In the provinces, power still rests in the hands of older men who acquired their political philosophy and administrative habits in the age of Stalin, or younger men who prefer the old heavy-handedness to the new subtleties.

We can illustrate this by the following anecdote. The head of the Writers' Union in Stalingrad in 1960 was one such old-timer, with the power to make or break young authors. When I asked him if there were any promising young writers in the region, he told me this story: "There's this young engineer who works on the new Volga hydroelectric project. He came to us at the Union sometime ago and said, 'I've written a novelette, and I should like to have it published in the regional magazine.' We read his work carefully, and then called him in. 'You write very well indeed,' we told him, 'and we should like to publish your novelette. But we feel that the Party officer in your story is not positive enough. You rewrite the ending, to make him a positive figure, and we shall be delighted to publish your work.' Well, do you know what this fellow did? Without changing a word, he sent the novelette to a Moscow magazine, and they published it without changes. Sometime later he came back to us and said, 'I've had my story published in Moscow, and now I'd like to have it published here.' And we said to him, 'We're delighted that Moscow has published you, and we'd like to do the same. But first you change the ending.' So the young fellow revised the ending as we suggested it, and we published it." And Soviet industry is an incredible mixture of the obsolete and the advanced, of yesterday's inefficiencies and tomorrow's automation. One need only pick up an issue of *Pravda*, *Izvestia*, or *Ekonomicheskaya Gazeta* to be confronted by this startling contrast between the age of space, nuclear power, and cybernetics and the wasteful and even primitive enterprise that would have gone bankrupt in the West but is kept in operation in the Soviet Union.

It is against this background that one must observe the new society—the scientific trail-blazers, the opinion-molders, the engineers, and even the vast corps of middle-grade technicians. This new society is demanding, sophisticated, restless, materialistic, questioning, eager to exchange ideas both at home and abroad. It was scarred by Stalin's barbarism far more than the West imagines or the Soviet leaders will concede. This, indeed, is the explanation of the profound "Fathers vs. Sons" debate of the past few years. In this dialogue, which has involved the highest Party leaders, the younger generation has been demanding of its elders a moral and political accounting. "What were you doing in the dark years of Stalinism? Did you protest or resist? And if not, how can you expect us to admire or follow you today? The questions have been general and damaging enough to compel even Nikita Khrushchev to explain and justify. But the young remain dissatisfied, and, both privately and publicly, the bitter dialogue continues, and it forms one of the most fascinating facets of Soviet life.

This is only one of the conflicts and contradictions that divide the new society. After Stalin's age of illegality, in which all Russia seemed to lie awake at night waiting for the sharp rap of police knuckles on the door, the Soviet citizen today craves order and legality. Arbitrary police action has been proscribed, and Western notions of justice have begun to seep into the legal codes. So great has been the revulsion against the police that the militiamen have often found themselves unable to gain compliance from the citizenry. By 1962 and 1963, it had even become necessary to wage a major propaganda campaign to persuade the public that the policeman was really an upstanding person, dedicated to justice and legality.

But even as the new society yearned for legality, the moral code that it developed sanctioned a breach of law. Indeed, the individual in the new society has developed two distinct moral codes. One serves him in his relations with people in his circle. The other one is employed in dealing with the Party, the state, and the sundry bureaucrats. Because of the low incomes and the régime of scarcity, it has long ceased to be immoral to cheat the state. The Soviet press itself is replete with tales of plant employees, from floor-sweeper to managers, entering into a conspiracy to gain higher pay or bonuses through fraudulent book-keeping. Such fraud upon the State produces no sense of guilt or even of acute embarrassment. Indeed, it is excused with the proverb, *Nye ukradesh, nye prozsivezh*, "If you don't steal, you don't survive." To protect itself, the state has now revived the "Control Committees" of an earlier generation, and these snoop, denounce, and expose. But even their efforts are defeated by the double moral code, and, as a result, the state has reintroduced the firing squads to halt what are euphemistically known as "the economic crimes."

Such chicanery is widely condoned when practised against the state; it is condemned when practised against a friend or neighbour. The state, even while frowning on the *anonymki* (anonymous denunciations) of the Stalin era, expects every citizen to do his duty by reporting his co-worker's wrongdoing. But public ostracism may be the fate of the man who does so.

In this topsy-turvy world, man's attitudes towards authority and towards fellow man are not alone in a state of flux. The sex mores are changing, from rigid puritanism to something approaching the free ways of, say, West Germany— or of Hungary and Poland. The attitudes towards property, labour, and the use of leisure have also changed.

UNDER STALIN, society was immobile. It yearned to move, but the state kept it stationary. It was frozen in its jobs, for labour mobility lowered productivity. It was frozen in residence, for housing was scarce, and no man could consider lightly moving to another city or town where he might find no housing. The only large-scale peacetime migration was involuntary. It was produced by the deportation of perhaps as many as ten or twenty million people to the sparsely inhabited areas in the north, in Siberia and in Central Asia.

This immobility is vanishing. Like the Americans in the nineteenth century, the Russians are on the move. True, millions in the urban centres, such as Moscow, Leningrad, or Kiev, use every stratagem to remain where they are. University graduates, assigned to jobs in remote areas, never reach the farms or factories to which they have been posted, or flee back to their cities at the first opportunity. Millions dream of life in the major centres, with their joys and comforts, with bigger stores, better transportation, and wider opportunity. But such dreams are not universal. The enterprising and the ambitious young man now goes east, to explore, build dams across the great Siberian rivers, lay railroads, build towns, search for minerals in the Altai Mountains, study cosmic rays in the Pamir, plan and build the second and third industrial complexes in Siberia. Much of Soviet citizenry is thus on the move—restless, searching for new horizons, seeking material reward or glory.

The Party is not happy about its footloose citizenry. It welcomes those who go east. But it is seriously perturbed by those who will not stay on the job, by the *letuny*, the shiftless workers. Since the Stalinist methods will not work, the Party early in 1964 proposed a new device—the so-called "labour passports," in which the portrait of a man as a worker and a citizen would be drawn. With their record thus exposed to public scrutiny and ridicule, the *letuny* presumably would hesitate to hop from job to job and town to town. Even the "labour passports," however, are not likely to stifle the new society's freshly acquired—and treasured—habit of mobility.

AFFLUENCE AND REVOLUTION are incompatible bedmates. This is why the growing affluence in the Soviet Union is such a significant factor both at home and abroad. The political myths and clichés of Soviet society deal with revolution. But reality ignores the revolution. The new society dreams not of world upheavals and barricades but of new apartments with "Scandinavian-type furniture and "imported" (if only from Poland) chintz curtains. The élite collect the abstract paintings and sculpture that they are required to denounce publicly; the less affluent aspire to own a *dacha*, a television set, a refrigerator, a motorcycle, if not an automobile. The state discourages this sense of acquisitiveness, but at the same time, it blandly sponsors lotteries offering rich material prizes, including works of contemporary art.

The new society has had to work hard to arrive at its present affluence, and it has had to make awesome sacrifices. But today it will not heed appeals for more sacrifices for the sake of future generations. It demands rewards for its labour and its inventive genius. And it treats official pleas and explanations with cynicism and even anger.

The affluence, or near-affluence, is not universal. In the Soviet Union, as in the United States, poverty is a grave problem. Perhaps a third of the Soviet population lives on the edge of penury. With free medical service and low rents, these underprivileged people nevertheless eat and dress poorly and go without even minimal comforts. However, in the Soviet Union, as in the West, the general level of livelihood is rising. The process is slow, as it must be in a half-agricultural, half-urban society, but it is unmistakable, working its magic to produce a social metamorphosis.

The mathematics of this new society are fascinating. Some fifteen million people in it describe themselves as specialists. The year Stalin came to power, the Soviet Union had fewer than 50,000 engineers; at the end of 1960 there were more than 1,100,000. In the same years, the number of doctors has risen from 63,000 to 400,000; of economists from a few thousand to nearly 200,000; of university-trained teachers and librarians from 60,000 to 1,380,000. By 1962, the number of scientists had risen beyond half a million. And, as its membership reflected the change in society as a whole, the Communist Party now included on its roster 50,000 men and women holding the degree of doctor of science.

This complex society no longer allows the Party to mold its mind. And it listens—as Russia of the Tsars listened a century ago—to its poets, writers, critics, playwrights. Once again, the poets are the guardians of Russian conscience and the brave spirits who ask the unaskable questions. Thousands come to hear them at the Moscow Sports Palace, at school auditoriums across the land, and at poetry readings in town squares. The university students memorize Yevtushenko's poems; the young engineers on a great power propect passionately declaim Voznesensky's work; and, in Kiev, two nationally known intellectuals tell me of weeping as they read Tvardovsky's long poem on the Soviet Union and Stalin. If the Party will deny there is anti-Semitism in the land, Yevtushenko will give them the lie, and millions will memorize his "Baby Yar," and Shostakovich will put it to music. If the Party will insist that "the cult of personality" has been eradicated, the same Yevtushenko will say what everyone knows—that Stalin's heirs are still in seats of power. If the Party will boast of bringing Socialism and the twentieth century to the countryside, Solzhenitzyn, in stories of almost Tolstoyan power, will show how the villages are still immersed in nineteenth century ignorance and bigotry.

The Party leaders rage and threaten. Inevitably, each period of thaw alternates with an icy storm. But the thaws now last longer, and repression which could be so savage in the early 1950's would be far more difficult to enforce in the mid-1960's. When an anti-intellectual campaign springs out of the obscure depths of the party *apparat*, intellectuals now dare to raise their voices in protest (as Ilja Ehrenburg, Yevgenii Yevtushenko, and others did in 1962). The protests can no longer be ignored—and the protesters can no longer be quietly eliminated *en masse*.

The intellectuals—the writers, the physicists, the space ship builders—do not yet have direct political power (even if a few seats are allotted to them on the Party's Central Committee). But their influence on the policy-making is undoubted, and it is exercised through channels whose variety is not realized in the West. Indeed, there is evidence of pressure groups lobbying for their particular causes, whether it is continued nuclear tests or, incredibly, an opportunity for a medical quack to demonstrate a magic cure for cancer cases called incurable by medicine. The machinery of governing remains wholly undemocratic. But the rulers already find it necessary to listen, to make concessions to public opinion (as Stalin rarely did), and to behave as if they were American politicians on a perennial campaign trail. Just as the nature of the relationship between the Soviet Union and other communist countries has changed, so has it changed between the governed and the governors within the Soviet Union itself—and for the same fundamental economic, political, and social reasons.

It would have been simple for the men who succeeded Stalin to continue with the machinery and methods they themselves had helped the tyrant to fashion. But they were intelligent enough to know that the new society would no longer tolerate what it endured under the lash of fear. It was, thus, pressure from this society that brought about the closure of the political internment camps from Kola to Vorkuta to Norilsk; that ended the Star Chamber trials and the existence of the secret police as a state within a state. One need only read the debates going on in the legal journals to see how public pressure has humanized the legal code. And it is again the new social pressures which now permit the space scientists to ignore their Party seminars, or allow students in leading art schools to dabble in abstract painting, or lead to the publication of Kafka's stories, or enable a nuclear physicist to argue in a leading journal that Soviet scholars will not understand the development of Soviet society until they read Freud as well as Karl Marx.

IT CAN BE (and has been) argued that all these manifestations are unimportant, and that all that really matters is the fact that the Party élite remains in absolute control and that its goals remain unaltered. This, I believe, is a poor argument. The Party élite, it is true, is still in power, but it itself has undergone a profound change to match the changing face of the society it governs. The goals of this élite have also been modified or changed. And only those who miss the extraordinary complexity and subtlety of the process of governing in the Soviet Union can argue that the élite wields absolute power. In post-Stalinist Russia, the governors must seek at least a measure of consent from those they govern.

Inevitably, the change in society must be reflected in state policies and attitudes. A startling illustration of this is provided by the conflict between Moscow and Peking. The breach may be explained in terms of traditional national rivalry, or of a struggle for primacy in the world communist movement, or even of personal dislike that Soviet and Chinese leaders bear for each other. But surely the fundamental reason for the breach must lie in the divergence of interests between a modern industrial state and society on the one hand and a still backward agricultural nation and society on the other. Half a century or more of industrial and social development separates the Soviet Union and China, and it is this gulf that the two communist parties cannot bridge. Out of this gulf spring their differences on war and peace, on the atomic bomb, on revolutionary strategy. The new Soviet society todays knows of revolution only by hearsay—and it has become persuaded that an ill-timed revolution somewhere in Asia or Latin America may well lead to nuclear war. The Chinese leaders and society are still in the midst of their own revolution. When they observe the underdeveloped world, they see in it all the conditions that existed in China less than a generation ago, and they exhort the starving peasantry of the have-not continents to follow the Chinese example. If the leaders of industrial Russia are preoccupied with peace, the leaders of agricultural and backward China are still obsessed with revolution. And, unlike the Soviet leaders, they dismiss the nuclear bomb as a military "gadget," the latest refinement in weaponry, that cannot possibly affect the fundamental laws of Marxism and revolution. Back in 1947, Mao Tse-tung told me, "We're too backward to fear the atomic bomb." The attitude has not changed since—whereas the Soviet leaders and society, who have built 100-megaton bombs and know their devastating power, are seeking to avert a nuclear disaster.

The communists have misappropriated many good words, and robbed them of virtue. Thus, too, with the words "peaceful co-existence." But it is futile today to recall the broken pledges and the misused phrases of the past, for an eternity—and the harrowing experience of the Cuban crisis —separates then and now. Even today, peaceful co-existence does not mean that the two rival political faiths and systems would somehow end their struggle. It does, however, mean that the rival systems are being driven by the compulsions of the nuclear age literally to co-exist in peace—for the alternative will be accepted neither by Western man nor by the changed Soviet society.

The Soviet Union is not likely to give up the historic power contest in which it is engaged. It, after all, is a great power, and it behaves like one. Just like other great states, it will continue to extend its influence throughout the world. But its overriding interest must be self-preservation in the nuclear age—and this imposes restraints on its action. It can provide military aid to Cuba, Indonesia, and Egypt. But it can chance no venture which might involve the risk of nuclear disaster. And this, inevitably, requires some sort of political arrangement with the West.

A change in attitude is also mandatory for the West. It, too, is subject to the restraints imposed by the H-bomb. But more than that, it cannot proceed on the naïve assumption that nothing has changed in the Red world—that Soviet society is the same today as it was in the fearsome 1930's; that Stalin and Khrushchev are alike, and so are their methods of governing; that the communist world is monolithic; and that the states of Eastern Europe are still the subservient satellites they were in the early 1950's. Those who insist that nothing has changed are blind to the magnitude and portents of the social and political change in the communist world. Worse, they do a disservice to the West by denying it the flexibility of attitude and action that the changed scene demands. It is only when we in the West understand the scope and nature of the change in the Soviet Union and the Red world—from a dull-witted Russian boy who will not be a cobbler to the breach between Moscow and Peking—that we shall be able to meet intelligently the challenge posed to us by communism.

The Soviet Viewpoint on Co-existence between States with Different Social Systems

THE HON. IVAN F. SHPEDKO

WE ARE HERE CONCERNED with one of the main problems of our time—the problem of peaceful co-existence between states with different social systems.

And now allow me to voice my considerations on the problem. Our points of view may be different, but that should not be an obstacle to an exchange of opinions. A good discussion, a frank exchange of opinions, is a very useful thing, and, of course, truth is born in the course of discussion. I would like to begin with several facts directly connected with the question of peaceful co-existence.

It is an undeniable fact that at present the world is divided into two different social and political systems, the capitalist system and the socialist system. The relations between these two systems leave much to be desired. I am sure you know this as well as I do.

It is a fact, too, that with the present level of the development of science and technology, with the present nuclear weapons and rockets, a world war would only lead to unheard of destruction and loss of life. According to the estimate of scientists and military men, so many of these deadly weapons have been stockpiled in the world now that there are enough to destroy the world several times over.

It is also a fact that the distribution and balance of forces in the world arena at present make it possible to eliminate world wars. They are no longer inevitable. The two different social systems can co-exist peacefully. This fact, too, does not need any special proof. Indeed, we are not at war, which means that we actually co-exist peacefully.

It was not so very long ago that some people would not even use the word "co-existence." You may remember the name of one rather well-known political figure in the West who once said that whenever he hears the word "co-existence" he has an impulse to reach for his gun. But the logic of life proved to be stronger than the emotions of such political figures. Now the idea of peaceful co-existence is generally accepted. It is the concern of every thinking man. It is generally accepted today that peaceful co-existence is an objective necessity. As regards the Soviet Union, the principle of peaceful co-existence was put forward by the great Lenin when the country was born, and since then it has been the general line of the foreign policy of the Soviet government.

What is peaceful co-existence? How do we understand it? Allow me to give this example: every one of us, wherever and however he lives, has neighbours. Sometimes you do not like your neighbour. You do not want to visit him, you would rather never see him at all, but you remain neighbours and go on living as neighbours. Indeed, what else can you do if neither wants to leave his home and move to another place? The same can be said about relations between neighbour states with different political systems.

It would be ridiculous to think that one country could be so antagonistic to another that the latter would move to Venus or Mars. That is out of the question. What is to be done then?

There are two ways out: either war or peaceful co-existence. And if you don't want war, you must find a way to live in peace with your neighbouring country, whether you like it or not. You must co-exist with your neighbour. That is the only alternative, for we all live on one planet. In short, peaceful co-existence means abandoning war as a means of settling disputes. It is peace instead of war. It is understanding and the establishment of normal relations between neighbouring states instead of hostility and violence. Peaceful co-existence is not only a pledge of non-intervention, but also an undertaking by all the states not to violate the territorial integrity and sovereignty of another country in any form or under any pretext.

On December 31, 1963, in the interests of peace, the Chairman of the Council of Ministers of the U.S.S.R., N.S. Khrushchev, sent a message to all heads of state. It was suggested in the message that an international agreement should be signed by all states, renouncing the use of force in settling territorial disputes and border conflicts. The Soviet government has posed the question of territorial disputes in view of its particular importance. In the present situation, any local frontier clash may quickly develop into a thermonuclear war. The message suggests concrete methods to solve territorial disputes, such as negotiations, mediation, and also other peaceful means in conformity with the United Nations Charter. The conclusion of a treaty suggested by the Soviet Union would be a serious step forward on the road to eliminating wars from the life of mankind.

The principle of peaceful co-existence does not at all require from any state the renunciation of its established system and ideology. One should not identify the problem of ideological struggle with the question of relations between states. The main tenet of peaceful co-existence is to confine the struggle to the ideological level and not to resort to force to prove your point. And when we Russians say that in the competition of the two systems our system—the socialist system—is bound to win, we do not mean to interfere in other countries' affairs or impose our ideology and our way of thinking on anyone by means of force. Why prove one's righteousness by means of war? Let us check in practice whose system is better. Let us compete without wars.

The question may arise whether peaceful co-existence implies division of the world into separate regions with high fences. And also, what will things be like beyond these fences? Peaceful co-existence does not imply high fences or iron curtains. Nor does it mean just being neighbours who refrain from war. Peaceful co-existence can and must develop into peaceful co-operation and competition in the cause of satisfying the needs of man in a more fruitful manner. Political and economic relations between states must be based on equal rights and the mutual benefit of the parties concerned.

Is this possible? Yes, it is quite possible. Take, for instance, the relations between the Soviet Union and Canada at the present time. Trade between our two countries is developing. Our cultural and scientific contacts are growing too. These are clear manifestations of the principle of peaceful co-existence between our countries.

Last year we in the Soviet Union had a very poor grain crop and we are pleased that Canada sold us more than six million tons of wheat. We understand that Canada is also pleased with the deal, as it has no doubt helped her in strengthening her economy. By the way, I can say that the fulfillment of the transaction is proceeding very successfully. Canada is a reliable trade partner and one whom it is pleasant to deal with. The wheat transaction has created a good atmosphere for further development of trade in the future. It is not for nothing that people say that the proof of the pudding is in the eating.

The cultural exchanges between our two countries are also growing. Soviet audiences highly enjoyed the performances in our country of Canadian artists and athletes—singers, actors, and sportsmen. I would even say that Canadian hockey players turned out to be good teachers for our own hockey players. I believe that the performances of Soviet actors in Canada also pleased Canadian audiences. It is true that some people are still prepared to take the Moscow circus bears for dangerous propagandists, but these misgivings are easily dispelled.

In conclusion, I would like to say that what has been done by our two countries in the fields of trade, sports, cultural and scientific exchanges, and in other fields as well—is not at all a limit. It is rather a good beginning, as the possibilities for both of our countries in these fields are enormous. These present manifestations of the principle of peaceful co-existence point to exciting possibilities in the future that cannot but be of benefit to both Canada and the Soviet Union.

SELECTED BIBLIOGRAPHY

BOOKS

BABB, HUGH W. (trans.). *Soviet Legal Philosophy.* ("20th Century Legal Philosophy Series," Vol. V.) Cambridge, Mass.: Harvard University Press, 1951.

BERMAN, HAROLD J. *Justice in the U.S.S.R. An Interpretation of Soviet Law.* Cambridge, Mass.: Harvard University Press, 1950. Revised, enlarged edition, New York: Vintage Books and Random House, 1963.

HAZARD, JOHN N. *Law and Social Change in the U.S.S.R.* London: Stevens and Sons, 1953.

———— and SHAPIRO, ISAAC. *The Soviet Legal System. Post-Stalin Documentation and Historical Commentary.* New York: Oceana Publications, 1962.

International Law Association. Report of the Fiftieth Conference, Brussels, 1962. London: International Law Association, 1963. (Proceedings and Debate on Juridical Aspects of Peaceful Coexistence, pp. 260–374).

KELSEN, HANS. *The Communist Theory of Law.* New York: Frederick A. Praeger, 1955.

KHRUSHCHEV, N. S. *An Account to the Party and the People. Report of the Central Committee, Communist Party of the Soviet Union to the 22nd Congress of the Party, October 17, 1961.* Moscow: Foreign Languages Publishing House, 1961.

KOZHEVNIKOV, F. I. (ed.). *International Law. A Textbook for Use in Law Schools.* Moscow: Foreign Languages Publishing House, 1962. First published in Russian in 1957.

KULSKI, W. W. *Peaceful Coexistence. An Analysis of Soviet Foreign Policy.* Chicago: Henry Regnery Company, 1959.

LAPENNA, I. *State and Law: Soviet and Yugoslav Theory.* London: The Athlone Press, 1964.

LAQUEUR, W., AND LABEDZ, L. *Polycentrism. The New Factor in International Communism.* New York: Frederick A. Praeger, 1962.

MCWHINNEY, EDWARD. *"Peaceful Coexistence" and Soviet-*

Western International Law. Leyden: A. W. Sythoff, and New York: Oceana Publications, 1964.

ROMASHKIN, P. S. (ed.). *Fundamentals of Soviet Law.* Moscow: Foreign Languages Publishing House, 1961.

SCHLESINGER, R. *Soviet Legal Theory. Its Social Background and Development.* 2nd edition. London: Routledge and Kegan Paul Ltd., 1951.

SKILLING, H. GORDON. *Communism—National or International? Eastern Europe Since 1956.* Toronto: University of Toronto Press, 1964.

VYSHINSKY, ANDREI Y. *The Law of the Soviet State.* New York: The Macmillan Company, 1954. First published in Russian in 1938.

ARTICLES AND PAMPHLETS

BERMAN, HAROLD J. "The Dilemma of Soviet Law Reform," 76 *Harvard Law Review* 929 (1963).

CRANE, R. D. "Soviet Attitude toward International Space Law," 56 *American Journal of International Law* 685 (1962).

GORE, A. "Principles of International Law concerning Friendly Relations among States," 47 *Department of State Bulletin* 972 (1962).

HAZARD, JOHN N. "Codifying Peaceful Coexistence," 55 *American Journal of International Law* 109 (1961).

——— "Coexistence Codification Reconsidered," 57 *American Journal of International Law* 88 (1963).

KRYLOV, S. "Les Notions principales du Droit des Gens," 70 *Hague Recueil* 411 (1947).

LAPENNA, I. "The Legal Aspects and Political Significance of the Soviet Concept of Coexistence," 12 *International and Comparative Law Quarterly* 737 (1963).

LISSITZYN, O. *International Law in a Divided World.* (International Conciliation Pamphlet.) New York: Carnegie Endowment for International Peace, 1963.

MCWHINNEY, EDWARD. "Peaceful Coexistence," 56 *American Journal of International Law* 951 (1962).

——— "International Law in the Nuclear Age: Soviet-Western Inter-Bloc, International Law," *Proceedings, American Society of International Law* 68 (1963).

———— "Le concept soviétique de 'coexistence pacifique' et les rapports juridiques entre l'U.R.S.S. et les Etats occidentaux," *Revue Générale de Droit International Public* 545 (1963).

MOSELEY, P. E. "The Meanings of Coexistence," 41 *Foreign Affairs* 36 (1962).

TUNKIN, G. I. "Coexistence and International Law," 95 *Hague Recueil* 1 (1958).

www.ingramcontent.com/pod-product-compliance
Lightning Source LLC
Chambersburg PA
CBHW020258030426
42336CB00010B/827

*9 781487 581015 *